SECRET CHEPSTOW

Louise Wyatt

AMBERLEY

Acknowledgements

Thanks to Wyatt Sisters Illustration for permission to use their images.

A heartfelt thanks for the support of my best friends: Mark (photographer, driver, cook and sounding board), Pooh and Kayla for the simple messages of support and pride. Love always.

First published 2018

Amberley Publishing
The Hill, Stroud
Gloucestershire, GL5 4EP

www.amberley-books.com

ISBN 978 1 4456 8133 7 (print)
ISBN 978 1 4456 8134 4 (ebook)

British Library Cataloguing in Publication Data.
A catalogue record for this book is available from the British Library.

Origination by Amberley Publishing.
Printed in Great Britain.

Contents

Introduction

It was a majestic magical building that first grabbed my six-year-old soul, beginning my lifelong love of history and buildings. Back then it was Dunster Castle in Somerset, so when I first saw Chepstow Castle it similarly took my breath away. It held that same all-encompassing air of mystery and fairy tale that had grabbed me as a child.

I am not local to Chepstow, nor currently an inhabitant, living nearer Newport after moving over the bridge from south Gloucestershire. I have visited Chepstow on many occasions over the years however, be it for the town itself or travelling the Wye Valley. I instantly loved the 'feel' of Chepstow, despite it being on a very busy commuter route. It has retained its 'olde worlde' atmosphere and I could almost feel the stories behind the buildings, which is why I wanted to research and uncover Chepstow's history for Amberley Publishing's Secret series, my second local history book for them.

The reader will notice I have not elaborated too excessively on the castle. This is because not only is there a myriad of information out there already, but because there is much more to Chepstow in the form of its architecture and industrial past shaping what it was. I was fascinated to discover that Thornwell – and not Chepstow, for example – was the area with the earliest archaeology regarding human habitation, and with no absolute proof of Roman settlement where modern Chepstow now sits, it was too good an opportunity not to write about.

Saying that, the castle is one of the best I've ever visited. The ruinous form still exudes a power and aura that must have seemed otherworldly when it was built and showed the Normans at their highest authority. It is most certainly an integral part of Chepstow, so I thought a brief history and a timeline would suffice for this particular book on the town.

What I found intriguing was the architecture that Chepstow has that still survives and the stories around its buildings; for example, the almshouses, the Town Gate, and the survival of so much of the Port Wall, which, even in the twenty-first century, is something to behold. From evidence of rich merchants, wealthy benefactors and religious history to the workhouse, Chepstow has a bit of everything. Workhouses have always drawn me in by their sheer Dickensian quality. While my imagination would love to run away with tales of dark, dastardly deeds, I managed to stay on track with the facts and only wish more of the building remained. And although it appears Chepstow Union Workhouse had a fair reputation, one cannot imagine having to live that life in our modern world.

I hope the reader finds the following an interesting journey into local history. Apologies if I have missed anything; the wealth and depth of information far exceeds the word count on this particular book.

1. Early Settlement

The earliest recorded settlement in the area is not actually the Chepstow we see today, despite the medieval ambience that still exists and the dominating feature of Chepstow Castle. In fact, the Monmouthshire Conservation Appraisal in 2016 states that there is very little evidence of prehistoric settlement. While Roman coins and pottery discovered around the area we know as Chepstow indicate Roman activity, there seems to be no evidence that a Roman fort (or any other Roman settlement) developed here – unlike at Usk and Abergavenny.

In late 1990/early 1991, archaeological field evaluations were carried out by the Glamorgan-Gwent Archaeological Trust Ltd (hereafter called GGAT) ahead of a proposed residential development in an area called Thornwell, just south of Chepstow. Excavations

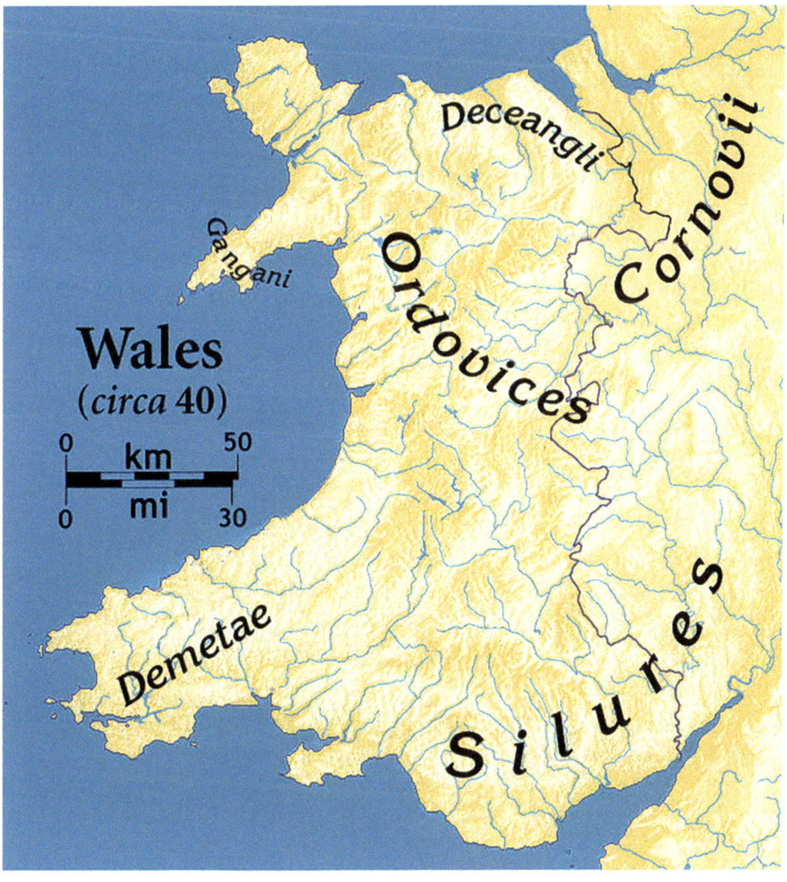

Wales at the time of the Roman invasion, with the modern Wales/England border for reference. (Courtesy of Notuncurious under Creative Commons 3.0)

of the then newly discovered large chambered tomb as well as a Bronze Age barrow suggest early settlement from the Neolithic era; discovered items include pottery and flints, as well as Romano-British earthworks – possibly a farmstead. It is rather sad to see what little remains of these archaeological wonders today, in their backdrop of a modern development.

DID YOU KNOW?
One of the very few rare occurrences of Roman finds in Chepstow was in 1895 when plumbing works were being carried out under Manor House in Bank Street. Bronze coins from the early fourth century showing the emperors Constantine I, Constantine II, Crispus and Constantius II (minted between AD 318 and 355) are now on display in the Chepstow Museum.

Looking up from the residential road towards remains of the Neolithic burial chamber, which is typical of a Severn-Cotswolds-type chamber, as described by GGAT.

Standing atop the chamber, looking back towards the road and out over towards the Severn Estuary.

A typical example of a Severn-Cotswolds-type Neolithic burial chamber from *c.* 3500 BC, Somerset. (Courtesy of Hugh Llewelyn under Creative Commons 3.0)

A bit further north from the chamber lies Bulwark Camp, which is now maintained as a public open space – approximately 3 acres – among another residential sprawl of twentieth-century housing. This was originally an Iron Age hill fort built by the Silures (the Celtic tribe that ruled in this part of Wales) and dates from 700 BC to AD 100. The Silures were known to be a very fierce tribe and successfully resisted Roman conquest, including defeating what was probably the 20th Legion in AD 52. Tacitus, the Roman historian who chronicled the invasion, stated:

> Conspicuous above all in stubborn resistance were the Silures. A naturally fierce people and now full of confidence … every warrior bound himself by his national oath not to shrink from weapons or wounds. Such enthusiasm confounded the Roman general. The river too in his face, the rampart they had added to it, the frowning hilltops, the stern resistance and masses of fighting men everywhere apparent, daunted him. Ostorius, worn out by the burden of his anxieties, died, to the joy of the enemy.
>
> Tacitus, *Annals*, Book XII, Chapter 30
> (www.sacred-texts.com)

The Silures were eventually subdued in AD 75 by the Roman general Agricola, Tacitus's father-in-law. According to John Davies in his *History of Wales*, the Romans believed a city was the key to leading a civilised life, so the Silures were granted a *civitas* (a social body of citizens who form a state) and Caerwent was born. The Roman name, Venta Silurum, means 'market town of the Silures' and is partially carried through in the Welsh version – Caerwent, meaning 'fortified placed with a market'. The medieval place name of Gwent is derived from Caerwent.

It appears from different sources that Chepstow may have superseded Caerwent as the main marketplace in the area. In his 1929 *History of Monmouthshire,* Sir Joseph Bradney states the foundation of Chepstow began in the seventh or eighth century after the abandonment of Caerwent. In 2008, Derrik Pratt states that Chepstow appears in the Llandaff Charter in *c.* 722 as '*Emricorua in guent iscoit*' – 'the busy place in Gwent Is Coed' (with 'Gwent Is Coed' meaning the kingdom of Gwent).

Although the Romans don't appear to have utilised Chepstow's geographical position as the Normans ultimately did, they established a river crossing further upstream. This took them from their main centres, such as Gloucester, onwards to their legionary fortress at Caerleon via the Wye's lowest defensible crossing. Before that time it is possible the Silures used Lanmelin wooded hill fort near Shirenewton (now looked after by CADW) as their tribal centre before the Romans came and established Caerwent, although CADW state there is no hard evidence to support this. In his 1950 historical booklet *Chepstow: Its Castle and Lordship,* Arthur Clark states that back in ancient times currents and tides may have made the crossing of the Severn to Beachley difficult. This is why the Romans used the Wye further up and possibly Portskewett too, which was also potentially used as a landing point for the Silures – Portskewett would have penetrated further inland than today; it is discussed in the next chapter.

Entrance to Bulwark Camp on the Wales Coast Path, Iron Age fort of the Silures.

Just inside the entrance of Bulwark Camp, looking out towards the Severn Estuary. Bristol is in the distance.

We are very lucky that majestic ruins of Caerwent still survive. They are breathtaking today, so must have been like something completely alien to the local tribal people. To date there have been no archaeological military finds or remains of villas in the surrounding area, pointing to evidence that this was a place built on unused land to keep the Silures subdued and away from the wild terrain that they had known best and which had served them so well previously.

DID YOU KNOW?
Remains of a Roman crossing over the River Wye were discovered by accident. In 1911, Dr Orville Owen, an American physician, was convinced that Sir Frances Bacon, the Tudor statesman, was the original author of Shakespeare's writings. His research sent him to excavate parts of the riverbed by Chepstow Castle for boxes of manuscripts. Needless to say, the search was fruitless and Owen died in 1924, and, seemingly, the idea with him.

Above and below: Caerwent south wall.

Caerwent south wall's plaque.

Thornwell Farm House

A short stroll away from the Neolithic burial chamber is a building one could possibly miss, even when looking for it. Situated down a slight hill among a small labyrinth of residential roads sits the Grade II-listed Thornwell Farm House.

An old well (visible on the first edition Ordnance Survey map, 1883) sits approximately 40 metres west of the farmhouse. Thought to be medieval in origin, the site was excavated in early 2007 ahead of planning application for a development of seventy-five dwellings.

After some clearance of modern rubbish and detritus, the well was located by GGAT. Finds from the well indicate a date of mid to late seventeenth century, with later modifications. Although not visible within the development today, it has been preserved in situ, meaning it is still in its original location. In 1956, when Thornwell was being inspected by the Ordnance Survey Archaeological Division and it was in its last throes as a working well/farm, the inspector was informed by the then owner – Mr Sharp – that the well had given its name to the farm due to a large thorn tree that had once been nearby, but was then long gone. According to local tradition, the water was a remedy for sore eyes and had been blessed at some point by a bishop of Llandaff.

DID YOU KNOW?
There are 200 scheduled monument sites within Monmouthshire: forty-six are prehistoric; ten are Roman sites, including four villas; four are early Christian sites; there are 101 sites from the post-Norman medieval period; and thirty-nine modern sites, including early industrial activities.

Thornwell Farm House from the Wales Coast Path.

Front elevation of Thornwell Farm House.

Thornwell Farm House back elevation, looking down from just below the site of the Neolithic burial chamber.

An interesting snippet about Thornwell appears in *A Stranger's Guide to Chepstow and The Wye* (1843):

> Another very retired and pleasing walk leads besides the Ancient Port and to the Manor of Thornwell, which comprises that ancient demesne constituting the right bank of the Wye at its embouchure. Here are the thorn and ancient well from which the place takes its name, an old manor house, and an arbour, where also you may get a very beautiful prospect of the Channel and scenery possessing features peculiar to itself.

Offa's Dyke

An outstanding feat of eighth-century engineering and planning, Offa's Dyke is often referred to as the original boundary between England and Wales.

Offa was the Anglo-Saxon king of Mercia from AD 757 to 796 and was the first whose charters used the phrase 'King of the English'. A successful warrior king, sources note his competent negotiating skills as well as his success in war. During his reign he was successful in pushing Mercia's powerful frontiers into Sussex, Kent, Essex and East Anglia. The name Mercia itself means 'marches' or 'borderland'; as the largest central kingdom in England at the time, Offa certainly had many borders to defend, including the one with Wales.

Offa's territory expanded from the Humber to the Thames and from Anglia to the lowlands of the Dee, Wye and Severn – thus, to the periphery of Wales. The Cornovii tribe had ruled the area called Powys, but by the year 600 had retreated to Pengwern (now Shropshire) due to Saxon colonists. Pengwern became the seat of the kings of Powys. In his *History of Wales*, John Davies notes how by the year 642 this too had been taken by Mercia, thus taking the Welsh lowlands. The men of the Welsh upland hills attempted to take back this land, specifically in 655, 705–07 and 722, albeit unsuccessfully.

DID YOU KNOW?
King Offa was the first king to introduce a monetary unit – the silver penny – with his image stamped onto it.

In 778 and 784 Wales was raided by Offa and Offa's Dyke was presumably built shortly after, over a few years. No one can really be sure if the whole linear length can be attributed to Offa (all 240 kilometres of it from Prestatyn to Chepstow!), just as no source is actually sure why it was a built – was it a defensive structure or an agreed boundary? Offa's charters often state 'fortress-building' as opposed to 'dykes' (dyke being Old Norse for trench or ditch). Natural defences were utilised as well as man-made earth embankments, showing defensive – not offensive – barriers within the dyke. Whatever it was originally intended for, it was an example of the power and cohesion of Mercia. In 1955, Sir Cyril Fox published a paper for Cardiff University suggesting there must have been a semblance of consultation with the kings of Powys and Gwent. Evidence for this theory shows up at Trelystan where the dyke is built to the east, thus leaving fertile slopes in the hands of the Welsh – hardly an offensive move. Near Rhiwabon, the dyke was built so the King of Powys retained possession of a fort. Respect was also shown to Gwent by building the dyke in such fashion as to recognise that the traffic and trading along the River Wye and at Beachley (there may have been a harbour there at the time) belonged to the kings of Gwent.

Within the next 300 years this ancient 'frontier' would be the basis for war, greed and bloodshed. It would most definitely become a boundary – an offensive one – becoming known as the Welsh Marches. Although Chepstow possibly replaced Caerwent as a marketplace, the Normans had arrived and after eons of prehistoric and tribal settlement all around Chepstow, the area itself came into a life of its own.

Offa's Dyke, showing the boundary between Wales and England and the power of Mercia. (Courtesy of Rushton2010 under Creative Commons 3.0)

2. Monmouthshire and the Marchers

Marcher Lands and the Normans

From around 1057, Gruffydd ap Llywelyn, the Welsh prince of Gwynedd and Powys, was recognised as the king of all Wales after having taken over Dyfed, Morgannwg and Gwent over preceding years. There had never been one ruler over Wales before (it had been ruled by princes of kingdoms) and there never would be again – Gruffydd was killed by the Anglo-Saxon warrior Harold, Earl of Wessex, in 1063, who then took control of Hereford and down the south of the River Wye.

According to the Anglo-Saxon Chronicle, when Harold was crowned King of England three years later in January 1066 he had been in the process of building a hunting lodge in Portskewett, approximately 4 miles south-west of Chepstow. Although difficult to picture now as the village is approximately half a mile inland, Portskewett (its name meaning 'harbour below the wood') was accessed by a tidal creek linking Portskewett to the River Severn. However, the prince of Gwent, Caradog ap Gruffydd, destroyed this building on the Caldicot levels and Harold never got a chance to retaliate as he was killed in the Battle of Hastings later that year in October. The Anglo-Saxon Chronicle (1065) notes:

> A.D. 1065. This year, before Lammas, ordered Earl Harold his men to build at Portskeweth in Wales. But when he had begun, and collected many materials, and thought to have King Edward there for the purpose of hunting, even when it was all ready, came Caradoc, son of Griffin, with all the gang that he could get, and slew almost all that were building there; and they seized the materials that were there got ready. Wist we not who first advised the wicked deed. This was done on the mass-day of St. Bartholomew.

In 2005, geophysical surveys of the aptly named Harold's Field behind the village church showed remains of ancient buildings. In 2007, the area was excavated by Channel 4's *Time Team*, where they found the remains of a fortified Norman tower house that was reached by the long-lost tidal creek; unfortunately no Saxon remains were found (these would have been wooden). When the area fell under Norman control, the area is recorded in the Domesday Book as being one of three dairy farms ('hardwicks') belonging to Chepstow Castle.

This was an example of showing the fortified buildings of the Normans. The Norman invasion of England in 1066 didn't affect Wales immediately. Offas's Dyke had previously been used as an unofficial boundary, a frontier with no fixed definition that had skirmishes along it between Wales and England. William was determined to subdue this turbulent territory. Chepstow was easily recognised as a strategic area to defend south-east Wales, with its low crossing point across the river and its location at the mouth of the Wye and Severn. This could enable the Normans to easily take control of the southern Marches and

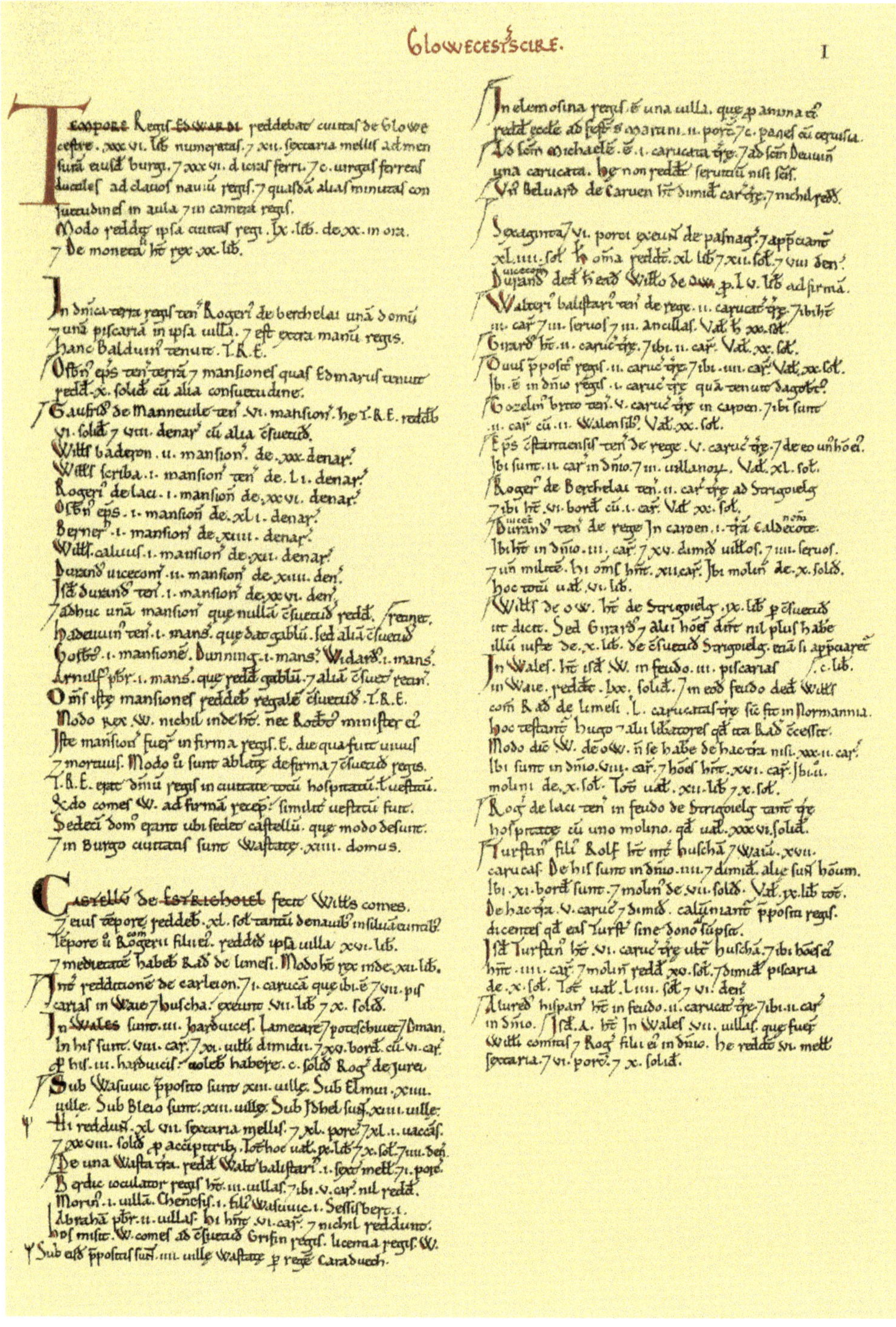
GLOWECESTSCIRE.

I

Gloucestershire's entry in the Domesday Book, including Chepstow (as well as Caerwent and Caldicot). It states Chepstow had nineteen households (medium) and fifty-nine *carucates* – very large areas of land that could be ploughed. (Courtesy of Professor J. Palmer and George Slater, www.opendomesday.org.uk)

river trade. While Portskewett has remains of a Norman fortified tower house, Chepstow got one of the first and most magnificent castles built. It still stands today – in ruinous glory – and will be discussed in a later chapter.

DID YOU KNOW?
The Normans were originally Viking invaders from Scandinavia. They were so powerful that the Frankish king ceded them land in northern France in the tenth century in dues for protection and to stop their raiding. This area became known as Normandy – Northmannia, land of the north men.

When William the Conqueror got to Wales, he found a country yet again ruled by princes of kingdoms. The Marcher lands ('march' meaning 'boundary/edge') now came into their own as William installed three of his most powerful lords at strategic points along the frontier, one of the first being his cousin, trusted boyhood friend, occasional deputy and long-time trusted right-hand man, William FitzOsbern.

FitzOsbern was given a new earldom – Hereford – and was the man who built Chepstow Castle, beginning as early as 1067. Around the same time, the new Norman earldoms of Shrewsbury and Chester were given to faithful followers by William the Conqueror. According to *The History of Monmouthshire: Volume 4, Part 1* by Sir Joseph Bradney (himself a High Sheriff of Monmouthshire in 1899), FitzOsbern went on the offensive in southern Gwent and the Forest of Dean, but no recorded tales of battle exist. This would lend to the idea that hardly any opposition reared up to the encroaching Normans. FitzOsbern went on to build Monmouth, Hereford, Ewyas Harold, Clifford and Wigmore castles. William I did not encourage his men to raid further into Wales, but neither did he stop them. Davies notes in his *History of Wales* that by 1081, however, William had no intention of annexing Wales and it appeared none of its kingdoms had much future. By 1086, the superiority of the Norman invaders of south-east Wales was showing: they had established castles at Chepstow, Monmouth and Caerleon, as shown in the Domesday Book, and William FitzOsbern had also managed to crush the kingdom of Gwent. Davies notes that although the Welsh knew their land inside out and had had mounted warriors for generations, not only did the Normans have superior armour, horses and arms, they were 'colonists of genius'.

DID YOU KNOW?
Wales has the highest concentration of castles in Europe, totalling between 500 and 641, depending on what source you read. Many are now ruins or visible earthworks, but in his book *Castles of the Marches*, John Kinross lists 116 castles along the Marcher lands alone.

Monmouthshire

Chepstow today sits within the county of Monmouthshire along with areas such as Magor, Caldicot, Abergavenny, Usk, Raglan and Tintern to name but a few. Monmouthshire itself wasn't formed until the Laws in Wales Acts 1535 and 1542 under Henry VIII. It was one of five new shires, the other four being Denbighshire, Montgomeryshire, Radnorshire and Brecknockshire. Marcher lord powers that had existed since the Norman invasion were abolished and officially, Wales was annexed to England.

So what brought about this change and the abolishment of the Marches, a cause of so much fighting and bloodshed for the previous 400 years or so? In 1509, at the time of the death of Henry VII, there were only three powerful Marcher lords left: Charles Somerset of Chepstow, Crickhowell, Raglan and the Gower; Edward Grey in parts of Powys; and the Duke of Buckingham in Newport and Brecon. In 1534, the Bishop of Lichfield, Rowland Lee, was appointed the president of the Council of Wales and the Marches, an administrative body that had been formed in 1472 by Edward IV to govern the lands known as the principality of Wales. By this time, most of the Marcher lands were under control of the king and no longer regarded as being beyond the reach of royal power.

Lee, also nicknamed the 'hanging bishop', proceeded to reign with aggression and terror by allegedly hanging (and boasting about it) more than 5,000 Welshmen and 'five of the best blood of Shropshire' over a five-year period. In his *History of Wales,* John Davies suggests there could be one of two reasons the Welsh did not pursue an uprising, as the men of Yorkshire did in 1536 and the Cornish in 1549. Both of those particular uprisings were against the Reformation instigated by Henry VIII. The Welsh had no representatives in Parliament to challenge royal policies and no members of old aristocracy were left in enough numbers to offer a powerhouse worthy of contending. It is also possible that the Dissolution of Monasteries didn't reach into Wales with enough impact until 1538–49, when campaigns against pilgrimages were initiated, thus touching the lives of the lay person.

Therefore, Monmouthshire was an area born around 1536 from what had been known as the Marcher lands, as well as land added onto English counties, such as Shropshire.

DID YOU KNOW?

Under Tudor rule, in the second Act of Union, the new county of Monmouthshire was attached to the Oxford circuit of court assizes so was considered part of England. It is unusual in that Monmouthshire is often listed in old sections of records as 'Wales and Monmouthshire'.

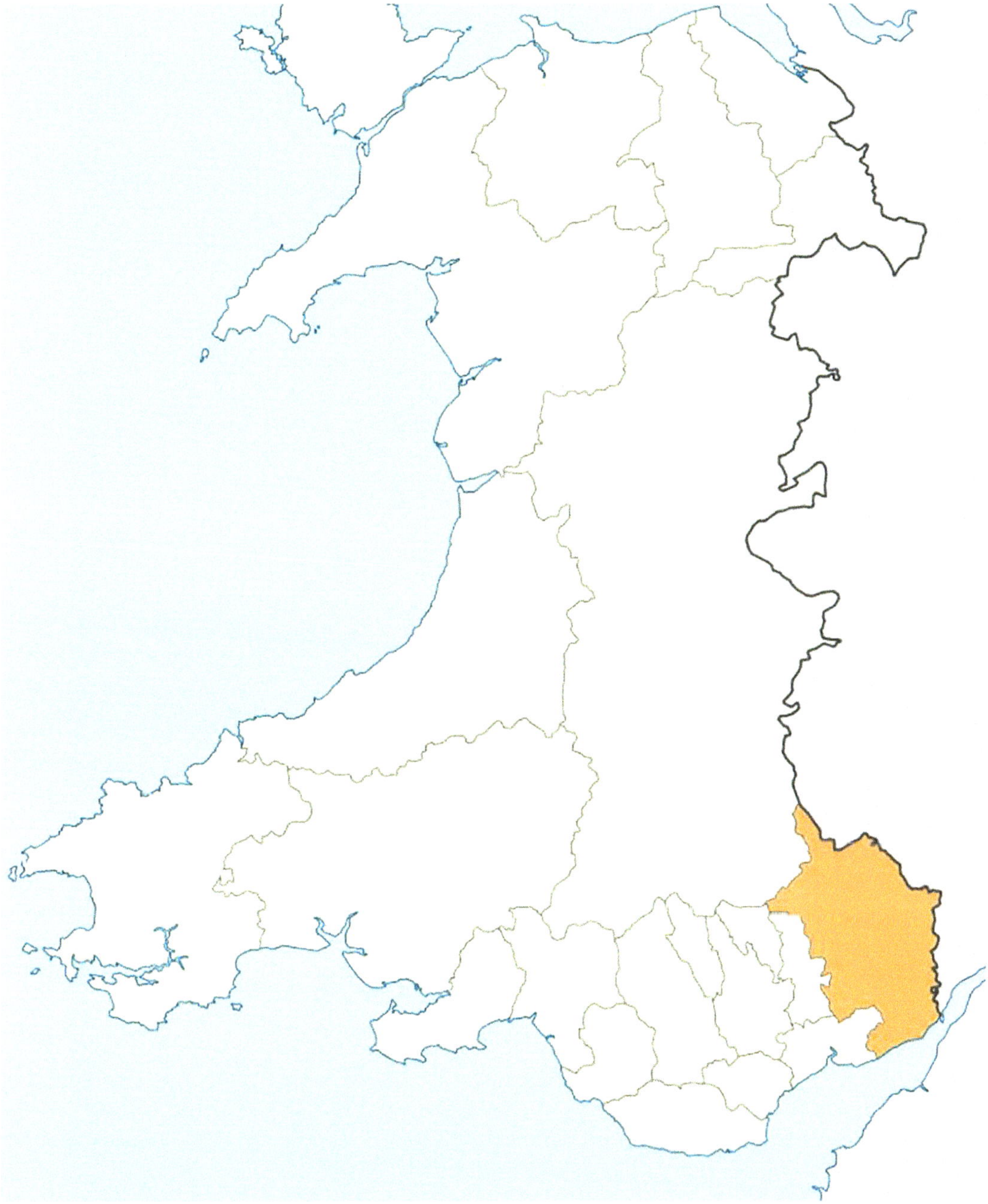

Monmouthshire in its position within Wales. (Courtesy of NordNordWest under Creative Commons 3.0)

3. Chepstow's Architecture

While the castle, in its most glorious setting, has to be mentioned in any book regarding Chepstow, this book aims to touch lightly on the origins and contruction. Not because it isn't worthy – far from it – but because there is a wealth of knowledge and books out there already dedicated to Chepstow Castle. *Secret Chepstow* could easily become another book on the castle, but Chepstow has other architectural treasures too. As such, this chapter shall cover a brief timeline of the castle before moving on to discuss the town's other historical architecture.

Chepstow Castle, viewed from Castle Dell.

Chepstow Castle

Begun in 1067 by William FitzOsbern, newly created Earl of Hereford, Chepstow Castle was originally a wooden motte-and-bailey structure (as was the earl's second castle at Monmouth), but later became one of the first castles to have a stone keep in Britain. As mentioned briefly in the last chapter, this particular area had been ignored by the Silures and then the Romans for a camp or settlement. The Silures had Bulwark Camp as their fort (as well as others at Lancaut and Piercefield) and the Romans had a river crossing further up the River Wye, en route from the powerbases such as Gloucester to Caerwent and Caerleon. This may have had a lot to do with geology and harbours that no longer exist as well as tidal currents.

DID YOU KNOW?
As well as Chepstow Castle's Great Hall being reportedly the oldest stone keep in Britain, the wooden castle doors are from the time of William Marshal – 800 years old, the oldest in Europe. Up until 1962, the doors were still hanging in the main gateway, but they are now housed safely in an exhibition on-site.

The Normans – especially FitzOsbern – changed all that. The speed in which Chepstow Castle was built signals its strategic importance. Chepstow was known by the Normans as Striguil (from the Welsh 'Ystriguil', meaning 'bend in the river') and by placing a defence here not only was FitzOsbern stating power and authority, he was showing status, engineering and battle genius. He also built the castle within easy access of another that was built very quickly, at a low crossing point of another powerful river trade route: Bristol Castle. FitzOsbern was also given lands in Oldland, Bristol, after the Conquest – now within South Gloucestershire. Bristol Castle also started life as a wooden motte-and bailey-defence, but went on to become one of the most powerful strongholds in England. David Sivier, in his book *Anglo-Saxon and Norman Bristol*, notes that FitzOsbern supplied Striguil (Chepstow) Castle from Bristol as water navigations were vital due to the difficulty of land travel. Nearly half of all the new towns built by the Normans were by the important ports, rivers and estuaries so supplies were adequate to keep the Norman dominance consistent. Twenty-four of the new towns in Wales were built on the coast and their supplies were from England via ship.

Year	Milestone of Chepstow Castle
1067–71	William FitzOsbern begins new defences in a motte and bailey style after being named Earl of Hereford by William I in recognition of his loyalty. FitzOsbern died on the battlefield of Cassel in Flanders in 1071.
1071–75	FitzOsbern's son, Roger of Breteuil, inherits Chepstow but is imprisoned after partaking in a rebellion to displace William I, thus Chepstow reverts to the Crown.
1081	William I visits Wales only once and establishes a mint and castle at Cardiff. More recent theories now ponder that it was William I who established the building of the great stone keep at Chepstow, not FitzOsbern. It is similar in build and design to William's White Tower at the Tower of London and the palace keep at Colchester.
1115–76	The fourth son of William I, Henry I, grants the lordship of Chepstow to the de Clare family. The death of Richard de Clare in 1176 (historically known as Strongbow) leaves his daughter Isabelle as one of the wealthiest heiresses in the kingdom. She became a ward of Henry II and Chepstow again reverts to the Crown.
1189	Isabelle de Clare is married to one of the greatest figures in British history: William Marshal. He becomes lord of Chepstow as well as all her other lands. He also begins the second major phase of building work at the castle including the gatehouse, lower bailey and the south-west tower.
1219–48	Marshal dies in 1219 and so begins the inheritance of the Marshal sons. Strangely, they all die with no heirs and in 1245, it passes to their sister Maud. In 1248 Maud dies and Chepstow passes to her son Roger Bigod 4th Earl of Norfolk. And so begins the ownership of the Bigods.
1270–1306	Roger dies in 1270 and Chepstow is inherited by his nephew, also called Roger. He starts the next biggest building programme of the castle. In 1284, Edward I visits and Martens Tower (possibly originally called Bigods Tower) was begun shortly after. In 1306, Roger dies and Chepstow reverts to the Crown.
1312–1403	Edward II grants Chepstow to his half-brother, Thomas of Brotherton, and much repair work is undertaken. Thomas of Mowbray, Earl of Norfolk, garrisons the castle against Owain Glyn Dŵr in 1403.
1468–1645	The Herbert family and their descendants, the Earls of Worcester, hold Chepstow, with some modernisation to the castle. Civil war breaks out in 1642 and Chepstow is taken by Parliamentarians in 1645.
1648–68	The Royalist Sir Nicholas Kemeys takes Chepstow but is killed when it is retaken by Parliamentarians. Chepstow is granted to Cromwell and money is spent on repairs and enforcements.

1668–1953	After the restoration of the monarchy in 1660 under Charles II, republican Henry Marten is found guilty of regicide and imprisoned in Martens Tower in 1668 until his death in 1680. Various building works continue over the years under esteemed families such as the Beauforts and Lysaghts. In 1953, Chepstow is under the guardianship of the State.
1953–84	Chepstow is under the care of the State until 1984 when CADW take repsonsibility.
1984 to present day	Chepstow continues under the care and responsibility of CADW.

Marten's Tower, on the approach to Chepstow Castle from the direction of the Tourist Information Centre.

View from Castle Dell.

Wentwood Forest, looking out across the Severn Estuary towards Bristol. Wentwood Forest was once part of the lord of Chepstow's royal hunting forest.

St Mary's Priory Church

When the Normans began to penetrate into Wales after the invasion of England, castle building was their forte to show dominance and lethal warrior power. However, the other way they showed their power was through religion.

Despite their prowess on the battlefield and their talent at invading they were faithful to the papacy in Rome, which had blessed the Norman invasion of England. According to John Davies in his *History of Wales,* the Normans were therefore horrified to find old ways of worship in the native Welsh churches (*clas*), along with wooden buildings, hereditary offices and married abbots. There was also no monastery following St Benedict, an influence that unified Latin Europe and to which the Normans abided by. The *clasau* (pleural of *clas*) were autonomous communities of clergy headed by an abbot. The Church in Wales website states of early medieval Welsh Christianity:

> As in other parts of Christendom, a distinctive spirituality emerged in each of the Celtic lands. Local theologies developed and particular aspects of the Christian faith were emphasized. This was the result of Christianity's interaction with the cultural, social and political environment of the local situation ... In his article on 'Celtic Spirituality' Thomas O'Loughlin (2005) notes that ... while the medieval West certainly had an image of its religious unity (expressed in maps, law and language) it had no experience of the actual uniformity in such matters as liturgy or the desire for uniformity in doctrinal expressions that characterise recent centuries.

To reiterate their power and in further subduing of the Welsh, the Normans replaced the Welsh *clasau* with ordinary parish churches and revenue transferred to monasteries, mainly situated in England. The Normans introduced Benedictine monasticism as soon as they could and, due to the importance of Chepstow Castle, by 1071 William FitzOsbern had established the Benedictine priory of Chepstow – one of the earliest. By 1150 there were eight Benedictine houses in Wales, mostly daughter houses of established abbeys in England or France. Although just a mile north of Chepstow, an Augustinian priory known as St Kynemark (Cynmarch, Kingsmark) appeared in records in 1270/71. Burton and Stober, in their book *Abbeys and Priories of Medieval Wales,* state the obscure origins of this priory and that its affiliation to the order of Augustine has long been questioned. The site is now covered by the housing estate Kingsmark Lane.

Chepstow Priory has the plaudit of being the earliest Norman priory in Wales, although it was also considered one of the poorest. It was a daughter house of Cormeilles Abbey in Normandy, France, which was founded by FitzOsbern in 1060.

DID YOU KNOW?
Chepstow Priory, built between 1067 and 1071 (now the Priory Church of St Mary's) was affiliated to the mother house of Cormeilles Abbey in Normandy, France. Cormeilles and Chepstow now have one of the oldest town twinning links in Europe.

Dovecote, one of the few surviving buildings of Cormeilles Abbey, founded by William FitzOsbern in 1060. (Courtesy of Nortmannus under Creative Commons 3.0)

What you see today of the church is a much reduced and altered version of the original. The church withstood the Dissolution of the Monasteries and remained a parish church as the nave had always been used for the people to worship in. The St Mary's guidebook, which can be purchased in the church for £2, states that there was probably a path originally from the castle directly to the priory. The choir aisles were demolished in the dissolution and an original central tower collapsed in 1701, destroying the transepts. In 1705–06 a new tower was built at the west end over the Norman doorway we see today. New transepts were added during 1838–41 when a new chancel was constructed, and around the same time – in 1841 – the nave aisles were demolished. A scheme to restore the Norman character went ahead in 1890, but after building works on the nave, chancel and south transept, the project was abandoned in 1913. Despite this rebuilding, some Norman masonry does survive: the remains of stone pillars behind the small alter, the font and the west (main) doorway.

Place de Cormeilles plaque in Chepstow.

In 1291–92, Pope Nicholas IV ordered the complete assessment of finances – both temporal (physical) and spiritual – of the parishes in Scotland, England, Wales and Ireland, known as the Taxatio Ecclasiastica. The pope had promised Edward I a tenth of the revenues to defray the cost of a crusade that Edward had promised to undertake. Chepstow was assessed in 1291 and, according to Burton and Stober in *Abbeys and Priories of Medieval Wales,* Chepstow had a value of £35 10*s* 11*d*. Of this, £15 13*s* 3*d* resulted from

St Mary's Priory Church, viewed from graveyard.

Sketch of St Mary's original Norman doorway by artist Lisa Wyatt. (Courtesy of Lisa Wyatt of Wyatt Sisters Illustration)

its temporal assets, which included 200 acres of arable land, pasture, forty sheep and seven cows. This would have all been within the Port Wall. The Taxatio Ecclasiastica remains an important document to this day.

Chepstow became independent from Cormeilles in 1452, having an English community as opposed to French. It was suppressed, however, as with many others, becoming a victim of Henry VIII's dissolution and ceased to be a priory from 6/7 September 1536. Today no trace of any priory buildings survive – the modern Tesco and associated car park cover the area.

Among the tombs at St Mary's is that of Elizabeth Browne (1500–65). She married the Earl of Worcester and became a lady-in-waiting for Anne Boleyn, Henry VIII's wife. Around the time of Anne Boleyn's execution, there were tales that Elizabeth Browne had helped smear her name.

Also buried here is Henry Marten, a close friend of Oliver Cromwell and a signatory to Charles I's death warrant. Martens Tower at Chepstow Castle was named after him – after the restoration of Charles II.

A glorious tomb of Margaret Cleyton is also here – the wealthy benefactor who gave much to the town of Chepstow. She established the George Inn and owned the Gate House adjoining the Town Gate. Her tomb shows her two husbands and twelve children.

Part of the graveyard on the north side of St Mary's, with eighteenth-century graves and Church Row cottages in the background.

Margaret Cleyton's tomb inside St Mary's Priory Church – note the figures along the bottom representing her two sons and ten daughters from both marriages.

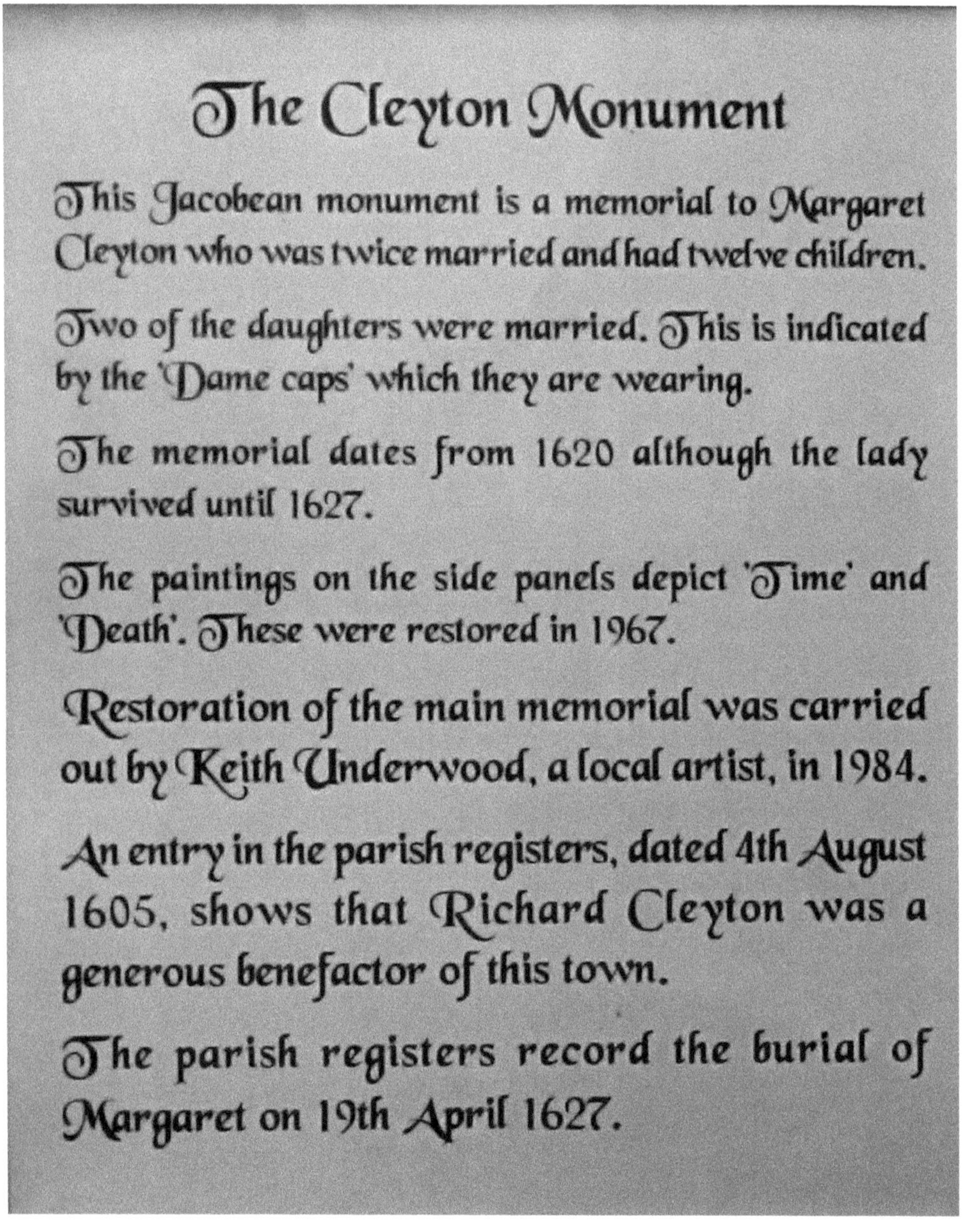

Plaque on the Cleyton Monument mounted on wall next to the tomb.

Port Wall and Town Gate

In 1270, the Marcher lordship of Striguil was inherited by Roger Bigod, 5th Earl of Norfolk, who was the grandson of Maud Marshal, eldest daughter of the great knight William Marshal. Roger made Chepstow Castle his main residence and proceeded with a building programme not only of the castle but also of the Port Wall and the Town Gate, both of which are still visible today.

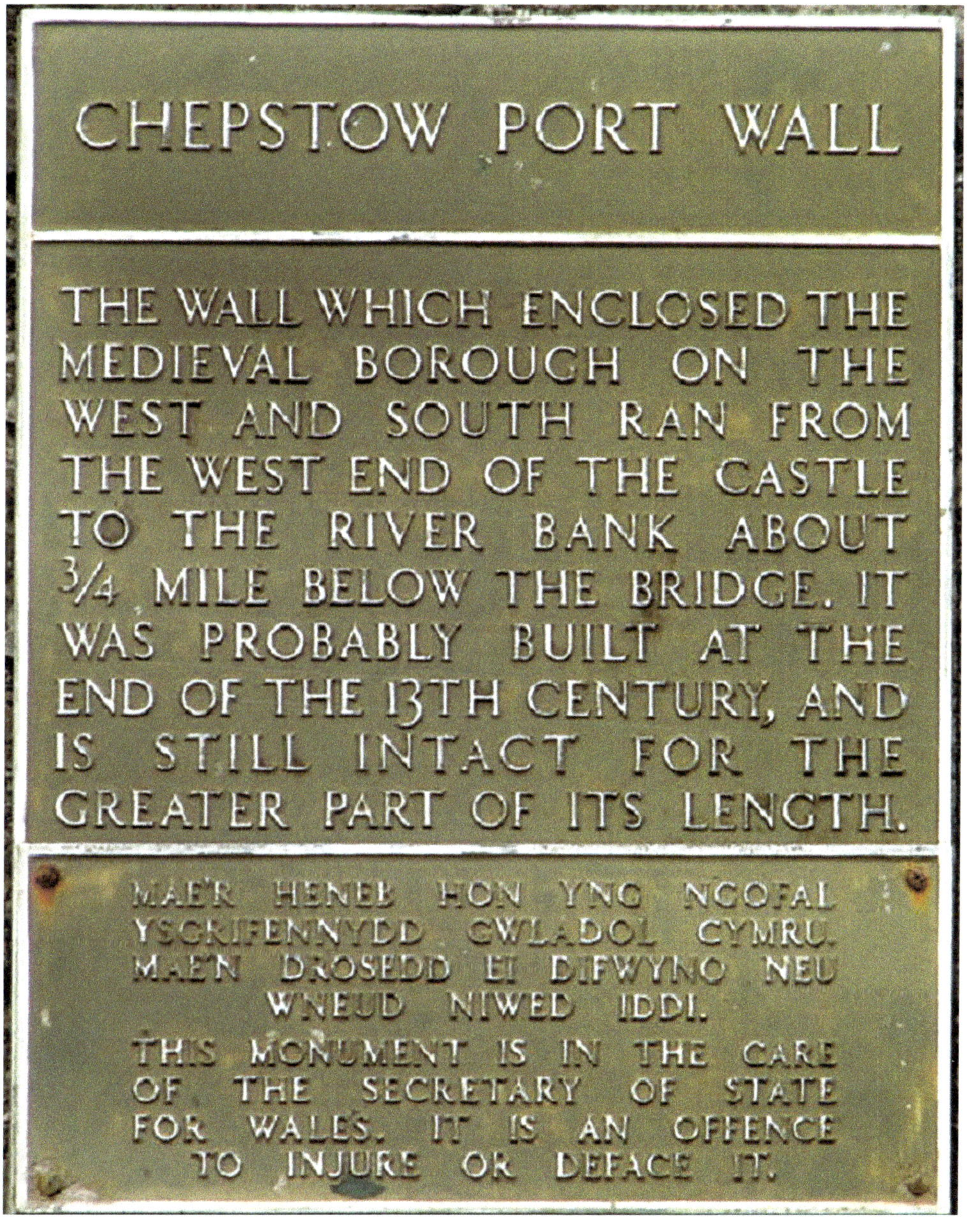

Chepstow Port Wall plaque. (Courtesy of Roy Parkhouse under Creative Commons 3.0)

With regards to the castle, Roger Bigod was responsible for the rebuilding/enlargement of the Great Tower as well as the tower now known as Marten's Tower, allowing comfortable accommodation for himself and his family. According to John Kinross in his book *Castles of the Marches,* this included building of the chapel and adding a kitchen and buttery as well as improving and extending living accommodation. On his history blog, author Stephen Spinks notes that these new chambers in the Lower Bailey were so highbrow at the time they became known as *gloriette* – a term used to describe living chambers in high-status residences from the twelfth century onwards.

With all this building at Chepstow going on, Roger Bigod also embarked on the Port Wall and Town Gate, both of which are Grade I-listed buildings and scheduled monuments. Although sources differ somewhat, on average the wall ran for approximately two-thirds of a mile and was around 6 feet thick and 15 feet high, effectively enclosing the natural promontory the castle stood on. There would have been eleven or twelve semicircular defensive bastion towers along the wall as well as the Town Gate, which allowed land access. Approximately 130 acres were enclosed *c.* 1294 including orchards and farms. Roger Bigod also granted the right of a market, which no one could enter without paying tolls to the lord – being Marcher land, the king was not paid any dues. It was at the Town Gate that the tolls were paid for taking animals and goods into the markets. It was rebuilt in 1594 by Charles Somerset, 1st Earl of Worcester.

DID YOU KNOW?

In 1508 the castle passed into the hands of Charles Somerset, 1st Earl of Worcester. He was cousin to Henry VII and Lord Chamberlain to Henry VIII. Somerset was the man responsible for the great pomp and ceremony of the famous Field of the Cloth of Gold, the meeting of Henry VIII and Francis I of France.

Gate House and Town Gate with an unfortunate traffic light spoiling the view! Closed in by modern buildings today, Gate House was built *c.* 1609 by local wealthy widow and benefactor Margaret Cleyton.

Above: Port Wall running left from the Town Gate to the breach for the A48, built in 1988.

Right: Where the A48 breaches – note the thickness of the walls and remains of one of the defensive towers.

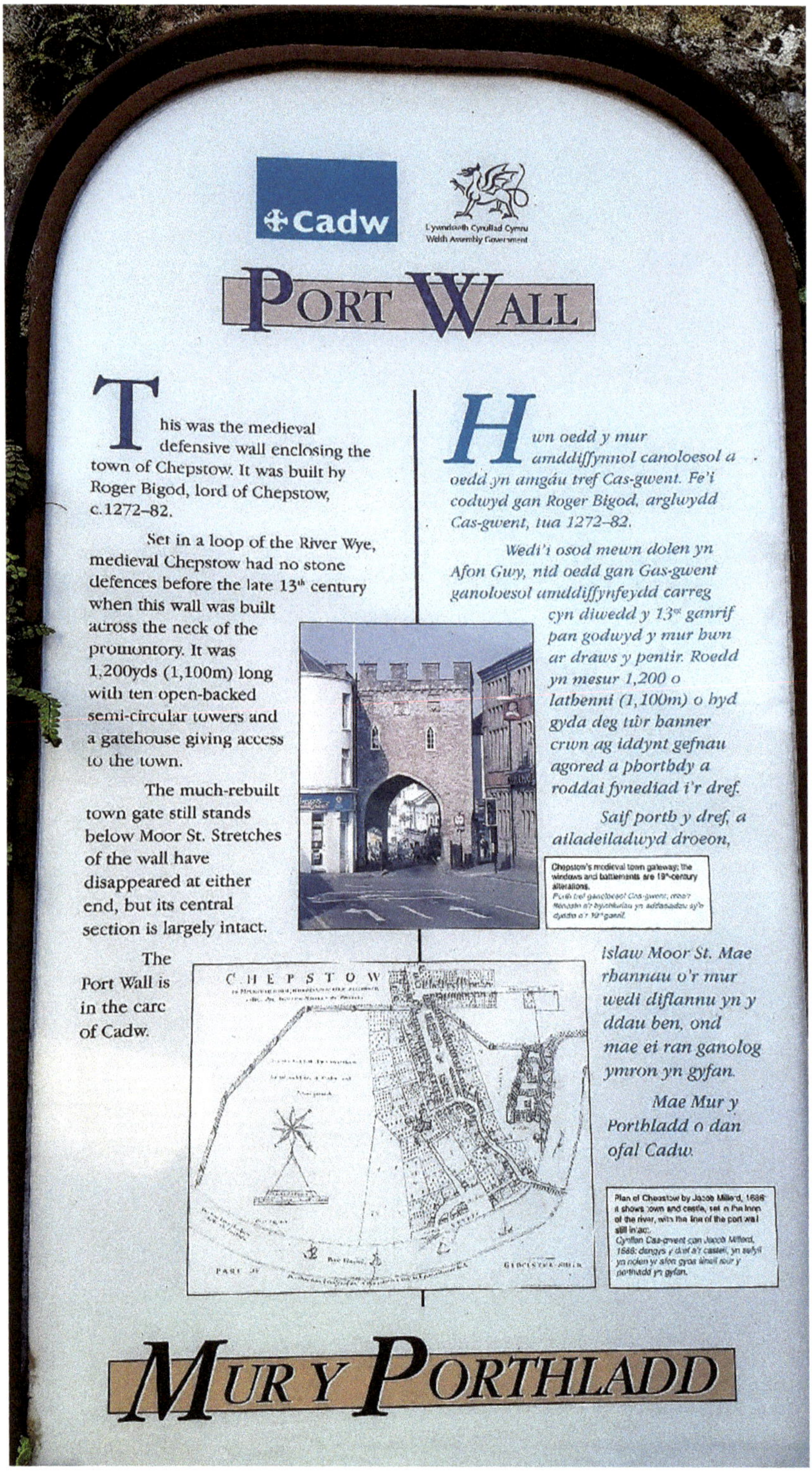

Port Wall plaque.

Gwy House

Gwy House was built for wealthy merchant and apothecary Warren Jane the Younger in 1796. Warren Jane was also a shipowner with numerous quays and warehouses, and according to Jenny Uglow in *In These Times: Living in Britain through Napoleon's Wars 1793–1815*, he had his fingers in a few pies: he owned two pubs (The Mermaid and the Sailors Tavern), co-owned a paper mill; and traded in timber, bark, wool and leather. The Sailors Tavern is now a Grade II-listed building in St Ann Street, running along The Back. He also lost two ships: one off the Cornish coast to the French (who reportedly used to loiter in boats just 2 miles off the Cornish and Devon coastline), and one to the Danes while trading further afield to the Baltic. He was also Justice of the Peace and a Freeholder of the County (a local government position).

In September 1762, Warren Jane the Elder and Warren Jane the Younger are listed as trustees for the Powis Almshouse. On Monday 21 January 1793, the *Gloucester Journal* reported the auction in Beaufort Arms, Chepstow, of a messuage (a house dwelling with land and outbuildings) in St Mary Street belonging to Warren Jane, soap boiler. In 1795 we have a Warren Jane listed as a soap maker and declaring bankruptcy.

During the mid-nineteenth century Gwy House was the property of a local surgeon called George Watkins, who married a daughter of Nathaniel Wells (as described in a later chapter). In May 1904, the *Chepstow Weekly Advertiser* announces a sale of furniture from Gwy House, including an Italian bedstead, antique silver, valuable oil paintings and

Gwy House today as Chepstow Museum.

mahogany dining furniture as well as outdoor items such as beehives, pea protectors and a croquet set. In 1907 Gwy House had become a boarding and day school for girls run by the du Bochet sisters. The headmistress was named as Miss G. du Bochet and the music teacher Miss A. du Bochet, and there were lessons in woodcarving, metalwork and bookbinding. Gwy House is again mentioned in the educational notices of the *Western Mail* in 1914, offering day and boarding for girls and 'preparation for the summer'. However, by 1915 it had become a Red Cross Military Hospital for the recuperation of wounded soldiers from the First World War – its then owner, Tom Valentine Ellis, managing director of Finch's Engineering Works in Chepstow, offered up his home Gwy House for use as the hospital as part of Chepstow's call to arms. In 1921 it became Chepstow District Hospital, and in 1982 it became the home – and still is – of Chepstow Museum.

Warren Jane family memorial, north-east of St Mary's burial ground.

Raglan Lodge

Raglan Lodge, a Grade II-listed building sympathetically refurbished and now a successful backpackers' hostel. (Courtesy of Ghmyrtle under Creative Commons 3.0)

A history plaque within the street paving outside the Raglan Lodge building.

Cromwell House

Cromwell House on Bridge Street, just up from the museum. It is possibly sixteenth century in origin with later remodelling and is claimed to be where Oliver Cromwell stayed after taking Chepstow in 1648.

Cromwell House sign.

Almshouses

Powis Almshouse as it is today. Built in 1721 by money left in the will of Thomas Powis, a vintner in Enfield, Middlesex, this almshouse was dedicated to twelve poor men and women of Chepstow. Thomas was born in Chepstow to a Grevill Powis, but not much else appears to be known about him. Built on land owned by John, Duke of Montagu, the almshouse is built on the remains of a medieval hospital and cellar. In his book *A History of Monmouthshire,* Sir Joseph Bradley notes there were eleven trustees to this charity, including a Thomas Lewis of St Pierre – the Lewis family were of Welsh descent and occupied the manor that is now a golf club and country estate, from *c.* 1400–1893.

Montague's Almshouse

Montague Almshouses.

Doorway to Montague Almshouse. Sir Walter Montague of Northampton was from a distinguished family of landowners and politicians and was one of twelve children. Walter's ties to Chepstow are through marriage to the daughter of Henry Morgan of Pencoed Castle in Llanmartin. Knighted in 1608, he was High Sheriff of Monmouthshire in 1608 and died in 1615, with his charity founded soon after. The almshouse was his own house and garden, eventually becoming more and more ruinous before being sympathetically redeveloped in 1958.

Hocker Hill Street, a steep cobbled street with a collection of Grade II-listed buildings. It was also called Hawkers Hill Street in the first edition Ordnance Survey map, noted by GGAT. At the top of the Beaufort Square end of the street, just to the right of this image, is a road sign with 'Hawkers Hill Street' on the wall.

Five Alls Inn is a Grade II-listed Georgian inn (with possibly earlier fabric). It may have previously been known as Crispin's Arms, but its current unusual name is taken from the sign: 'a soldier (I fight for all), a bishop (I pray for all), a king (I rule all), a lawyer (I plead for all), John Bull (I pay for all)'. The last figure is said to have originally represented the Devil, but this was replaced at the clergy's request, as noted by www.britishlistedbuildings.co.uk.

DID YOU KNOW?

The word 'apothecary' comes from the Ancient Greek *apothcea*, meaning a place where wine, spices and herbs were stored. By the 1200s it meant someone who stored and sold these items, and by 1430 it meant wholesale trade merchants selling 'en-gros' (the origin of the word 'grocer'). By the mid-1500s, apothecaries became the equivalent of modern community pharmacists.

4. Chepstow Port and Industry – Medieval to Modern

> The port of Chepstow was the only one in Gwent, except Newport, to which ships of any size could come. From here barges used to take goods up the river as far as Hereford. In 1791 there was a large trade, both import and export, shops of as much as 700 tonnes burden bringing wines from Oporto and deals, hemp, flax, pitch and tar from Norway and Russia. Timber was exported to Portsmouth, Plymouth, Deptford and Woolwich; bark, iron and cider to Ireland, Liverpool and other places.
>
> *Sir Joseph Bradney*
> *A History of Monmouthshire: Vol. 4, Part 1* (1929)

It is hard to believe Chepstow was once such a busy, bustling, international trading port. According *The Chepstow Story* by the Chepstow Society, a port developed in the town shortly after the Normans came to power; early shipping is mentioned in the Domesday Book of 1086, showing FitzOsbern receiving an annual levy from ships sailing upriver to the forest. Chepstow was historically an entrepôt of Bristol and thankfully the town prospered, not just because of its demography but also probably largely due to the fact duty payments went to the Marcher lordship and not the king. By the early fourteenth century, it was possibly the largest market town in South Wales. Indeed, in *A History of Wales*, John Davies notes that by 1300 the prosperous southern towns from Chepstow to Haverfordwest were sizeable and thriving. The first recorded mention of a market is in 1306, as noted by *Gazetteer of Markets and Fairs in England and Wales to 1516*.

DID YOU KNOW?
John Frost, William Jones and Zephaniah Williams were reputedly the last men sentenced in the United Kingdom to be hanged, drawn and quartered before it was abolished in 1870.

The Act of Union (a twentieth-century term) in 1536 more or less neutralised the power of the Marcher lords. With regard to the ports, in 1545 there was a sign of things to come when the Crown placed an officer in the port of Cardiff. Although the Crown had moved to incorporate all Welsh duties and customs within the English remit by 1559, as late as

1563 the collection of customs around South Wales was still being divided between the Earl of Worcester and the Earl of Pembroke, with Chepstow under control of Worcester. In 1573 there is the first recorded customs house in Chepstow where four deputies were recorded in 1578, thus showing the Crown's authority in superseding the Marcher lords, also noted in Duncan Taylor's thesis 'The Maritime Trade of the Smaller Bristol Channel Ports in the Sixteenth Century'. Incidents such as the steward of Chepstow threatening to pillory a Crown official in 1572 and the countess of Pembroke refusing to pay duties on imported hides in the early 1600s were a just couple of episodes of many where the Crown decided enough was enough. In his *The Port of Chepstow,* Ivor Waters notes it is possible the threat to the Crown official in 1572 possibly led to the first customs house appearing in Chepstow a year later.

The importance of Chepstow port was noted in Volume II of the Universal British Directory of Trade, Commerce and Manufacture (1792/3). In 1791 Chepstow was a busy national and international port trading in import and export – 700 tonnes of wines from Oporto (Portugal) as well as hemp, pitch, flax and tar from Norway and Russia. Every Tuesday a 70-ton market boat sailed to Bristol and returned on Thursday, and a stage waggon arrived from Brecon and Abergavenny every Monday, returning on a Tuesday. 'There are five constant trading vessels between this port and London which, in general, go and return every two months.' This is not including any local trade. A busy port indeed.

The Chepstow Society notes that between 1790 and 1795, Chepstow port handled a larger tonnage of goods than went through Swansea, Cardiff and Newport combined, including legitimate exports such as iron and wire from works at Tintern, just a short trip further up the Wye.

However, despite the port facing some decline in seventeenth century due to loss of Marcher privileges, the Chepstow Society also notes how industry such as coal mining developed further west into South Wales and trade was directed towards Newport and Cardiff as these ports were in a better location.

DID YOU KNOW?

The Defence of Realm Act 1914 gave the government powers to commandeer land and buildings, as well as prohibit normal peacetime activities such as flying kites, using or buying binoculars, starting bonfires, feeding bread to wild animals and discussing military matters on public transport.

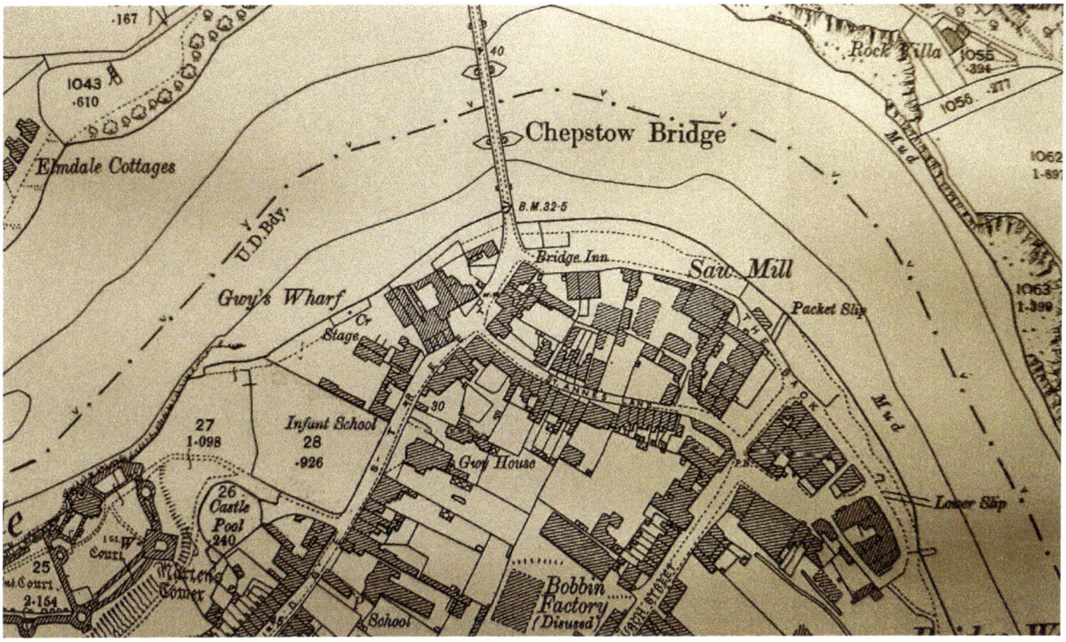

Various wharves and slipways, Chepstow, OS map, 1900.

The Back today, Chepstow's once heaving port and dockyard.

The Chartist movement lasted from 1838 to 1857 and had strongholds in northern England, the East Midlands and the South Wales Valleys. It was an early form of trade union. In 1832 the Reform Act allowed only those who held property to be able to vote, thus most voters were from the middle and upper classes. In 1834, the Poor Law forbid any working men from claiming outdoor relief, thus forcing working families into workhouses and being separated once inside. The Industrial Revolution had produced a mass workforce over the years and Chartists believed in a fairer democratic system and better living conditions for the working classes. These three men who sailed from Chepstow Port stood up and spoke out for the Chartist beliefs, leading men to Newport on an uprising that was bloody, violent and unfortunately ended in the Chartist defeat. John Frost, William Jones and Zephaniah Williams were convicted of high treason in November 1839 at the Shire Hall in Monmouth and sentenced to be hanged, drawn and quartered, a punishment first recorded in the thirteenth century and abolished in 1870. This was commuted to transportation for life and in 1856 all were given unconditional pardons. John Frost returned to Bristol to live with his daughter and died in 1877, aged ninety-three; he is buried in the city. William Jones remained in Australia as a watchmaker, dying in poverty in 1873, and Zephaniah Williams, a coal miner, discovered coal on Tasmania and founded the Tasmanian coal trade, dying in 1874 a wealthy man.

Timber

By the 1700s there were six royal dockyards: Portsmouth, Plymouth, Deptford, Woolwich, Chatham and Sheerness. The first royal dockyard was Portsmouth, commissioned by Henry VII in 1496. In 1513, Henry VIII built two more along the Thames – Deptford and Woolwich – in response to threats from Spain and France. Chepstow's port helped to supply the timber to four of these dockyards, which indicates its significant importance as a port. Between the years 1761 and 1768, there were 16,573 loads of timber delivered to the royal dockyards. Any timber not considered good enough quality for the ships was sold to local shipbuilders at Chepstow, Newnham and Gatcombe.

As seen in the section on Raglan Lodge in the previous chapter, John Bowsher was a local timber merchant who, according to an article by Mike Baker et al in *The Mariner's Mirror* (2002), was one of five timber merchants, known as a cartel ('cartel' in this sense simply means a coalition to promote a mutual interest), who supplied timber during the Napoleonic Wars. In his book *Napoleon: The Sword of Albion,* Dr John Sugden notes that in several articles Mike Baker suggests Napoleon visited Bowsher in Chepstow due to a deadlock between the timber cartel consisting of Bowsher, Larking, Hodges, Watkins and Stuckey, and the Admiralty. The cartels were blamed for having the monopoly on supply and pricing, but other factors such as limited availability of indigenous timber played their part. Admiral Lord St Vincent, a colleague of Nelson, attempted to enforce inspectors to curb the control the cartel had over the price of timber, which Bowsher – the Chepstow spokesman – vehemently opposed.

DID YOU KNOW?

When the new Standard Shipbuilding Company bought Finch's Yard as well as the extra land, they had to close local footpaths across the fields known as the Meads, as well as demolish part of the southern stretch of the thirteenth-century Port Wall along with cottages and the old Mill House.

However, in 2013, Andrew Helme, curator of Nelson Museum in Monmouth, states there is actually no evidence that Nelson stayed in Chepstow at all. It is known Nelson visited Wales – Pembrokeshire to be exact, where his friend Sir William Hamilton lived – and stopped off at the Forest of Dean in 1802 with regard to the timber supply for naval ships. Nelson was shocked at the amount of forest that had been cleared for charcoal furnaces and ordered a huge replanting of acorns for future oak trees. It was at this time that the naval dockyards were reportedly running low on timber for shipbuilding. Nelson's scathing report of the state of the Forest of Dean, where he discussed the mismanagement of the area and put forward remedies, is now housed in the Nelson Museum in Monmouth.

The timber trade slowly went into decline. Chepstow became a bonded port in 1830, meaning it could store the timber in a secure area and distribute/manufacture as needed. Two years later, in 1832, Newport also became a bonded port, but because Chepstow had no coal industry and local forests had become seriously denuded the town could no longer compete. Despite some minor timber trade, by 1844 wine had become more valuable to import and export.

Wine

In the sixteenth century Bristol was the second largest importer of wine in the country – London being the first. However, Bristol merchants imported their wine via Chepstow for avoidance of customs (equivalent of a modern-day tax haven). In his thesis, Duncan Taylor notes that in the years 1502, 1517 and 1526 large shipments of wine from Bordeaux were taken to Chepstow to be trans-shipped (decanted into smaller vessels) to escape paying the English dues that they would have had to pay in Bristol. There are still the remains of a wine cellar at pavement level underneath Powis Almshouses, which was used by various merchants during this time.

However, local wine merchants hadn't always been that lucky. In the twelfth century, Henry II gave his queen's native Aquitaine (Bordeaux is a city in this region) merchants the monopoly on the wine trade. Although this was a time when the de Clare's, the current Marcher lords, should have enjoyed no interference from the king regarding monies and privileges, Ivor Waters notes in *The Port of Chepstow* that there is no evidence to suggest Chepstow merchants benefitted either.

As such, wine had been an important chief import from the very start of this ancient trading port. In the thirteenth century, wine was shipped up the Wye for the king's expedition into Wales, and there are records of wine en route to Monmouth Castle being stored at Tintern Abbey at a charge of 2*d* a day.

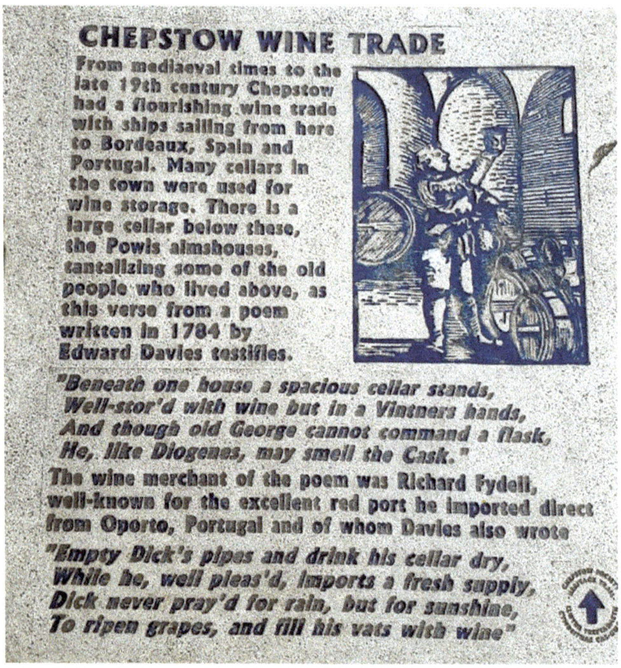

A Chepstow Heritage plaque embedded in pavement by the cellar door next to Powis Almshouse.

DID YOU KNOW?
The nineteenth-century novelist and journalist William Makepeace Thackeray is the great-great-great-grandfather of the comedian Al Murray.

In 1572, English merchants were still avoiding paying duty by using Chepstow to land their wine. Waters, in his *A Port of Chepstow*, notes the tale of two wine merchants – one from Exeter and one from Bristol – who had bought Gascon wine into Chepstow without paying the duty to the Crown (now Elizabeth I). A Crown official attempted to arrest the two men in Chepstow for evading payment and found himself being summonsed to the Steward of Chepstow, who happened to be the brother of the earl of Worcester, the current Marcher Lord. The Steward went on to call him 'a false knave' and threatened to nail the official to a pillory by his ears. It was this incident that probably initiated a customs house being built at Cheptsow, as mentioned previously.

Shipbuilding

Chepstow had a bustling and ancient shipbuilding history – Sir Joseph Bradney describes Chepstow as having 'ship-building from time immemorial and has been an important industry'. However, writing in 1977 in *The Port of Chepstow*, Ivor Waters notes 'there is no documentary evidence of ship building until the eighteenth century'. It could be safe to say that given river trade existed before the Norman invasion, as well as the strategic location, FitzOsbern deciding to build the castle and the fact a few miles over the water lay Bristol – the home of top-quality shipbuilding, immortalised in the saying 'ship-shape and Bristol fashion' – it is probable that more locally built ships existed before the eighteenth century. Indeed, *The Chepstow Story* states that by 1524 Chepstow had a shipbuilding history and there is even a plaque saying this on the Chepstow Town Trail

As previously mentioned, the port declined gradually over the decades but was briefly revived during the First World War with the National Shipyards Scheme. This consisted of Shipyard 1 (Chepstow), Shipyard 2 (Beachley) and Shipyard 3 (Portbury).

Edward Finch (1812–73), an engineer from Liverpool (where his father had established the Finch & Willey Foundry), won the contract for the ironwork of Brunel's Railway Bridge in 1852. Once this was completed, he decided to stay in Chepstow and developed Finch's Bridge Works at the site in Chepstow. The 1861 census showed Finch living with his wife Elizabeth, two servants and being an employer of seventy-six men and fifteen boys. Finch died in Chepstow in 1873 and his yard, Edward Finch & Co, continued to build bridges and ships in the 1880s.

During the First World War, especially by late 1915, devastating losses of essential food and fuel occurred due to the destruction of merchant shipping in the Atlantic. In *Shipyards, Scandal and Pigstyes* by the Chepstow Society, it is stated that up to 300,00 tonnes of shipping a month was being lost to attacks by German U-boats, who were lying in wait around the waters out of the Bristol Channel and around Ireland, just like pirates had done while waiting to attack the trade coming out of medieval Chepstow port all those years previously.

Chepstow Heritage Trail plaque situated in The Back.

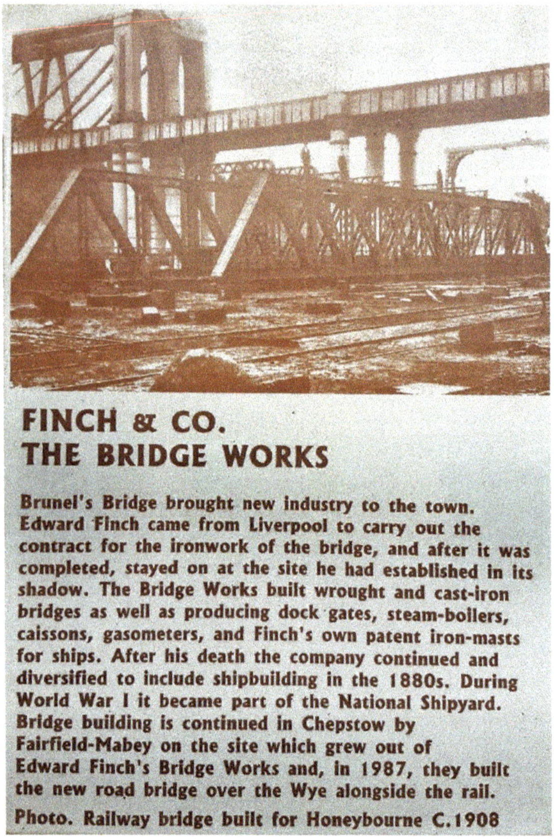

Chepstow Heritage Trail plaque on the current dock gates – now a building site for a housing development.

A local Tutshill man and former apprentice at Finch's Yard, John Henry Silley (1872–1941), helped establish a consortium of leading shipowners, and in April 1916 the Standard Shipbuilding Company was born. Silley had previously been a chief engineer in London for Star Shipping Line and was now managing director of Standard Shipbuilding Co. He was an advocate of a standardisation practice of building ships that was rapid and more productive than old methods. This company bought Finch's Yard by the railway bridge as well as a further 45 acres of open fields called the Meads, adjacent to Finch's Yard, for the amount of £300,000 (approximately £22 million today). The company renamed itself E. Finch in 1916 according to *Grace's Guide to Industry*; however, by June 1917, Great Britain had lost another 1.4 million tonnes of shipping to the Germans and as most attacks were around the Pembrokeshire coast, the government decided the Standard Shipbuilding Company were acting too slow. Under the Defence of the Realm Act 1914, the War Cabinet agreed to establish three national shipyards around the Severn Estuary – at Chepstow, Beachley and Portbury. The government also installed its own management.

DID YOU KNOW?
One of the many exports from Chepstow was high-quality paper used in the production of banknotes by the Bank of England.

It was not a popular scheme locally. The Admiralty commandeered the workhouse, displacing many elderly residents, and it was eventually closed in 1918. The Town Gate was threatened with demolition to fit in with remodelling the road system (which thankfully didn't happen) as well as the pier on the river being dismantled. Beachley residents – mainly farmers and fishermen – were given just a fortnight to leave their land. In instances where the Standard Shipbuilding Co. were building housing for their workers (such as Garden City), when the government took over building work slowed down. A new hospital was built called Mount Pleasant but the logistics of its use in comparison to where the shipyards were caused difficulties and anger at what was believed to be a waste of money. Chepstow Community Hospital is now near the site. It seemed that after the government took control of Chepstow's shipyard it soon became apparent that the opposite of what was planned – faster production and thus better defences – was happening: shipbuilding was proving unproductive and only one standard ship was ever launched from Chepstow (none from Beachley by the end of the war) and organisation frustratingly slow. Growing criticism came from politicians as well as trade unions, who were objecting to military labour. The war ended in November 1918 and while Beachley remained in government's hands, Chepstow came into the ownership of Monmouth Shipbuilding Company in 1920 and launched a few warships before closing in 1923. Fairfield Engineering and Shipbuilding Co. bought the yards and built bridges during the intervening years of the First and Second World Wars, but went bankrupt in 1966. Mabey Engineering took over until recently and today the site is being regenerated with the building of a new housing development.

According to Ivor Waters in his booklet *The Town of Chepstow,* the total cost for the government's not-so-productive National Shipyard Scheme was £6,120,000 – approximately £221 million today.

Salmon

Unlike the flabby fish in London sold,
A Chepstow Salmon's worth his weight in gold,
Crimps up delightful to the taste and sight,
In flakes alternate of fine red and white,
Few other rivers such fine Salmon feed,
Nor Taff, nor Tay, nor Tyne, nor Trent, nor Tweed.

Revd Edward Davies
Rector of Portskewett (1718–89)

Chepstow salmon had a distinguished reputation for its quality, excellent taste and sought-after supply. After visiting Chepstow around 1842 the author William Makepeace Thackeray noted the 'delightful town' and claimed that Wye salmon were the best in the world. According to Walker in the book *Fish – Food from the Waters*, salmon is freshest when caught in the estuary or shortly after its entry to a river, preferably during early spring. The quality of a natural salmon far outweighs the farmed salmon, with Wye salmon having a unique taste.

In 1790, the Duke of Beaufort was the Lord of Chepstow. This included possession of the fishing in the Wye from Brockweir to the mouth of the river, and large quantities of salmon were sent to London as well as places such as Bath, Bristol and Oxford.

DID YOU KNOW?
With a tidal range of approximately 40 feet, the Wye has the second-largest tidal range in the world, second only to the Bay of Fundy in Nova Scotia, which averages at 53 feet.

A reader's letter from *The Cardiff and Merthyr Guardian* from 5 July 1867 entitled 'Wye Salmon':

> Dear Sir - I am sure your readers will be glad to hear that a salmon weighing over 56lb. was taken in a net, on the 14th July., in the Wye, about four miles below Hereford. A fish of this great weight has never before been taken in that river within living memory. I may add that in April last a salmon, 391/2 1b., was taken with the rod near Rhayader, 50 miles higher up the river, and several unusually large fish of from 351b to 251b. very recently in the nets between Hereford and Monmouth in the sister river, the Usk, several fish of 31lb. to 241b. weight have been also caught by angling...

Above left: First line of Edward Davies' poem outside Barclays Bank, High Street, Chepstow.

Above right: Second line of Edward Davies' poem.

Other industries also flourished in Chepstow over the years, such as clockmaking, a bell foundry and bottle making. Eight of the ten bells in St Mary's Priory Church were cast by a local man named William Evans in the eighteenth century. He was the last of his family in this trade, however. He died in 1770 and has a memorial stone in the south transept of St Mary's.

Boscobell House in Welsh Street, adjacent to Castle Dell, is a Grade II-listed Georgian house. It is at the rear of this where Evans' bell foundry was, giving good access to the river port. This was especially useful as Evans' bells went far and wide – including the West Country and Lancashire as well as across the Severn to Bristol. Although a bell house is recorded here in 1605 and Evan Evans (father of William) was making bells in 1724, it is thought that the Evans foundry was the only bell foundry in the county and probably active earlier in the sixteenth century.

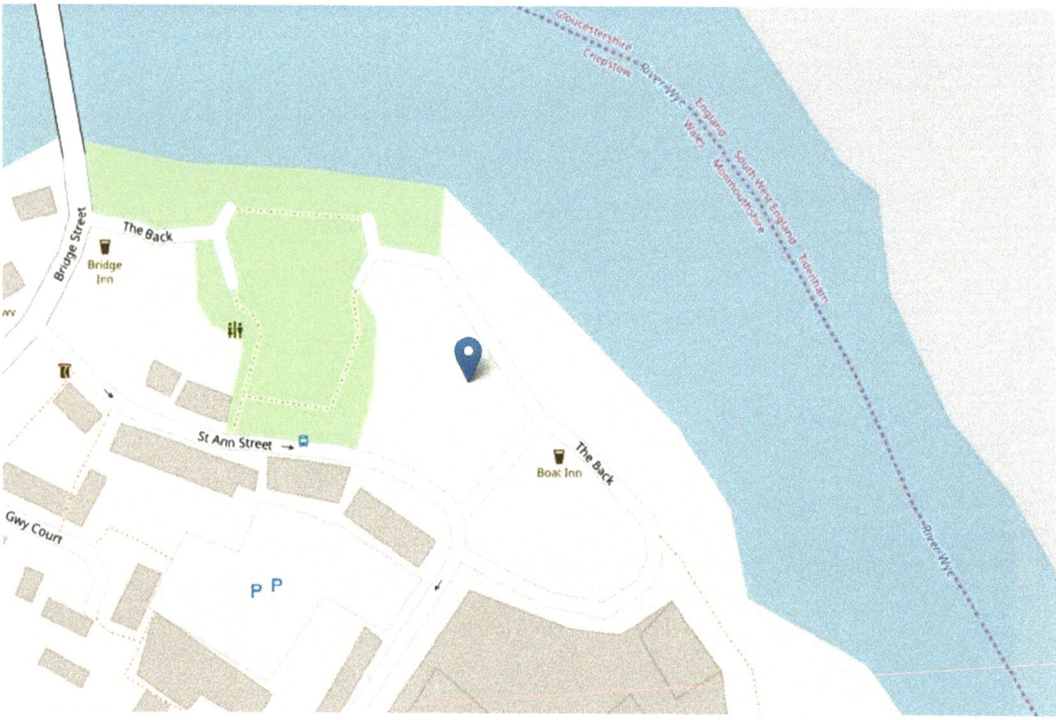

Site of the Grade II-listed Stuart House, nineteenth-century headquarters for Wye Fisheries. (© OpenStreetMap contributors under the Open Database License)

Stuart House today.

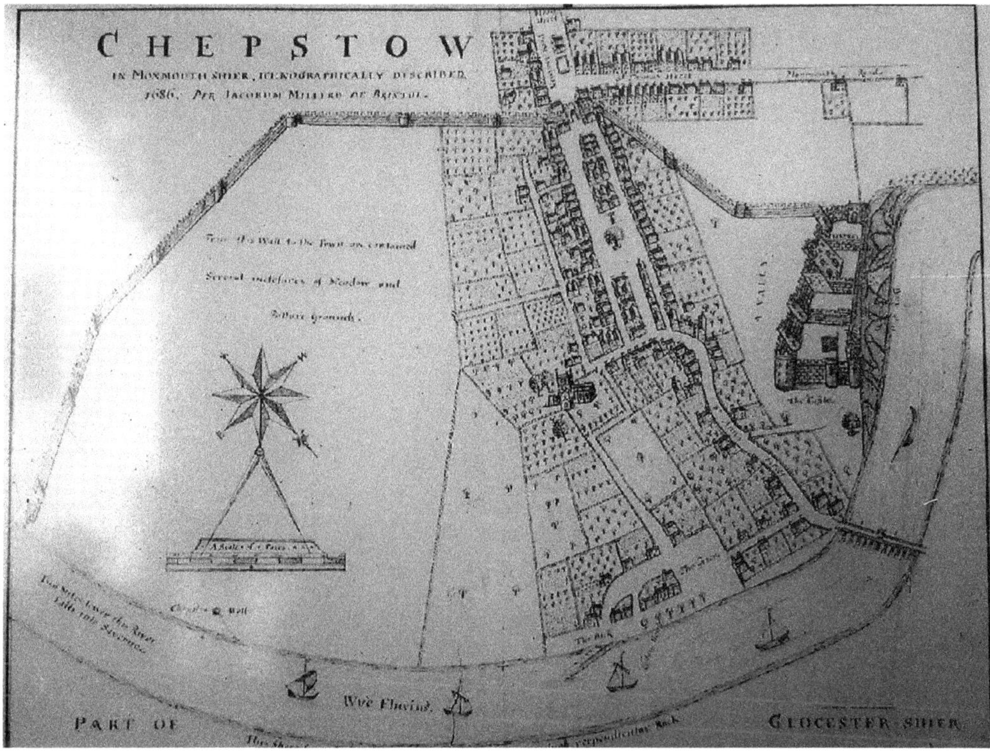

Right: Map of Chepstow, 1686.

Below: A Chepstow Heritage Trail plaque in the pavement outside the door of No. 23.

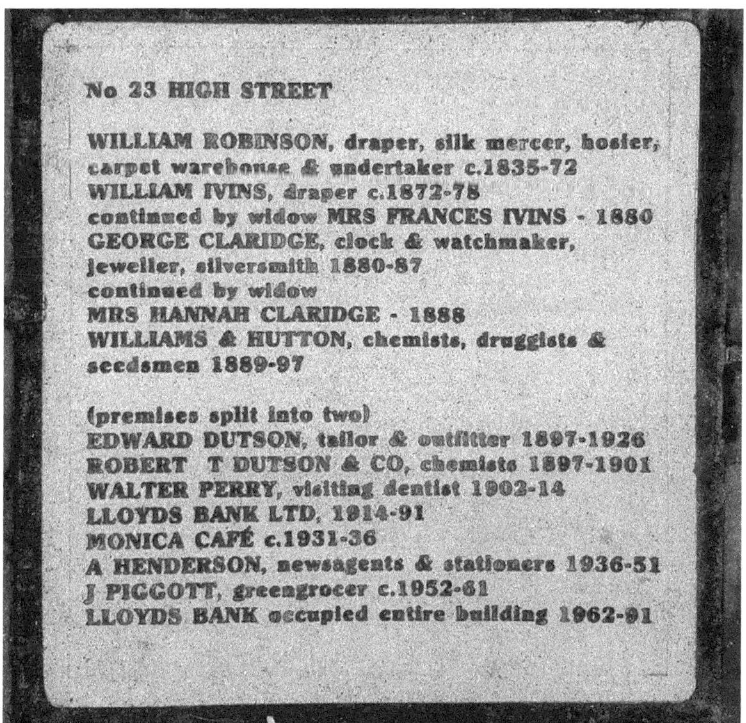

5. Chepstow Workhouse

In 1348–49, the Black Death decimated populations across not only the British kingdoms but across Europe, leaving a severe shortage of agricultural labourers among other workers. This saw the collapse of the feudal medieval social structure in England. Those that survived realised they could now travel to other shires and demand higher wages as there were no laws or customs to bind them as it had previously. In 1349, an Act called the Ordinance of Labourers was promulgated through Parliament in 1351 as the Statute of Labourers. It was the reaction of the ruling elite and aimed to fix wages at pre-plague levels and limit the freedom of movement of the able-bodied. It didn't work.

In 1388, the Statute of Cambridge came into force, which enabled Justices of the Peace of a hundred (a division of land within a shire) to have more power restricting the movements of servants, beggars and labourers. Servants and labourers needed permission to move outside their hundred or risk being put in the stocks. This Act also directed that the hundred be responsible for its own 'impotent poor' – the aged, infirm and incapable. In 1547, the Statute of Legal Settlement ordered cottages to be built for the impotent poor – possibly an early reference to an almshouse? However, it also branded and enslaved the able-bodied found begging. The Poor Act of 1552 declared that parishes collect alms to give out to the impotent beggars and keep registers of their poor, thus outlawing begging. The most comprehensive was the 1601 Act by Elizabeth I, which

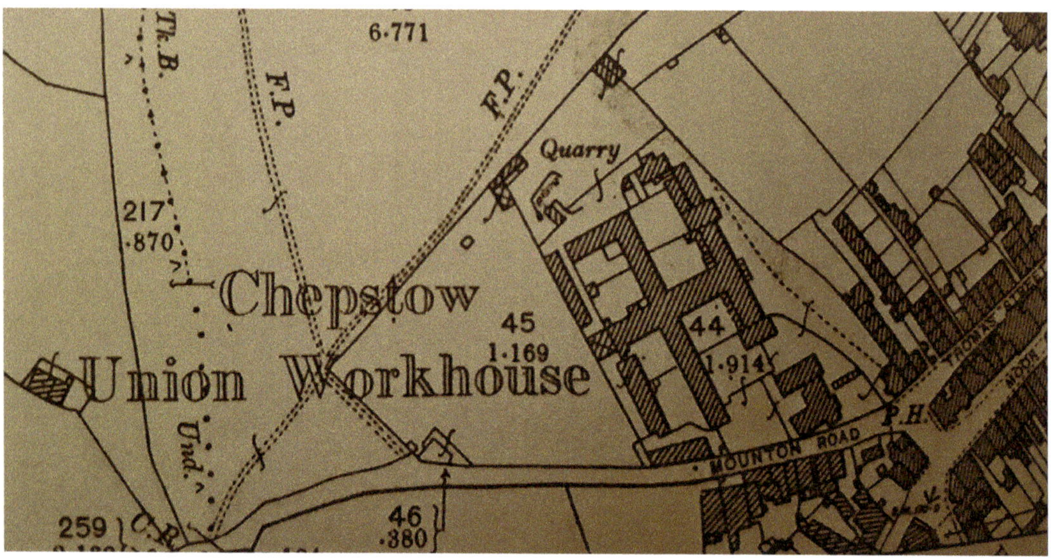

Plan of the workhouse, OS map, 1900.

aimed at providing 'houses of dwelling' (early almshouses), providing apprenticeships for orphans and providing labour for the able-bodied poor.

DID YOU KNOW?
Charles Dickens was an ardent support of the poor and lower classes, writing a piece in 1850 describing his walk around a workhouse. The language is descriptive and he notes at one point that a person may be better off in jail.

These principles were obvious in Chepstow with the establishment of Powis and Montague almshouses as well as benefactors such as Margaret Cleyton and John Bowsher. Alms would have been collected to help out the poor by providing outdoor relief such as money, food and blankets. In 1722, the Settlement, Employment and Relief of the Poor Act (also known as Knatchbull's Act or Workhouse Test Act) urged parishes to utilise workhouses by sifting out the irresponsible claims on a parish – only those most needy would enter a workhouse, which would provide shelter, food and work. Furthermore, in 1782, Gilbert's Act urged parishes that were responsible for their poor by law to form unions to share larger workhouses and offering poor relief jointly. It also changed the parish administration by introducing significant changes in the form of Parish Guardians. In 1836, Chepstow Poor Union was founded. This was a Board of Guardians from surrounding parishes – thirty-two in this case, including Shirenewton, Undy, Portskewett and Caldicot to name just a few – who came together to provide relief to those not able to help themselves; this would have included the old, infirm and orphans. The union had been able to do this by utilising Gilbert's Act of 1782 and two years after the union was founded Chepstow Union Workhouse was built on Mounton Road in 1838.

Life in a workhouse was extremely hard and only desperation would get people waiting to be admitted. Families were split up once admitted and children under seven years old were only allowed to stay with their mothers if it was expedient. Married couples were kept apart so they could not have more children, and inmates usually consisted of the poor, infirm, single mothers and orphans. Dr Marjorie Bloy in her article on *Conditions in the Workhouse* notes that a typical day starts at 5 a.m. and bed at 8 p.m., with work, prayers and meals served three times a day. Work consisted of repetitive tasks such as bone breaking, oakum picking, stone breaking and walking a corn mill. Meals often lacked nutrition, which led to illness and starvation. Chepstow would have been no exception, with its fair share of orphans and their hardship.

The Chepstow Union census of 1851 shows seven-year-old John Dutheridge classed as a pauper and scholar, so he was supported by poor relief and had schooling within the workhouse. There is no one else there at that time by the surname of Dutheridge so it is assumed he was an orphan. However, other records show the death of a Keziah Dutheridge in 1844 at Chepstow Workhouse. John's year of birth can be assumed to be 1843/4 due to his age in 1851. Keziah was only twenty-four at the time of her death and, according to the records, is buried in St Mary's. Further census records in 1841 show she had been a female servant at Lodge's Farm in St Briavels, Gloucester, aged twenty so it may be surmised this is the same woman. In 1843, she got herself incarcerated at Gloucester Gaol for larceny for stealing a loaf of bread. She may have got pregnant and admitted herself to Chepstow as a last resort, which would have been typical of that time. Could she have possibly died in childbirth, leaving John an orphan? This is something that is definitely worthy of more investigation.

In contrast, in Michael Greening's *A Family History* he states that Chepstow Workhouse was one of the better managed institutions, especially for children who were fed and educated as this was a lot more than could be said of children left to walk the streets. Schooling in Chepstow Workhouse was on-site from 1840 to 1880 when the children then began attending Chepstow Board School. Board schools were a precursor to modern state primary education. The original detached school building at Chepstow was used for the weekly Board of Guardians meeting.

According to Kelly's Directory in 1895, the workhouse school had become a chapel for inmates and the children attended the board school. From 1930 onwards the workhouse became Regent House Public Assistance Institution.

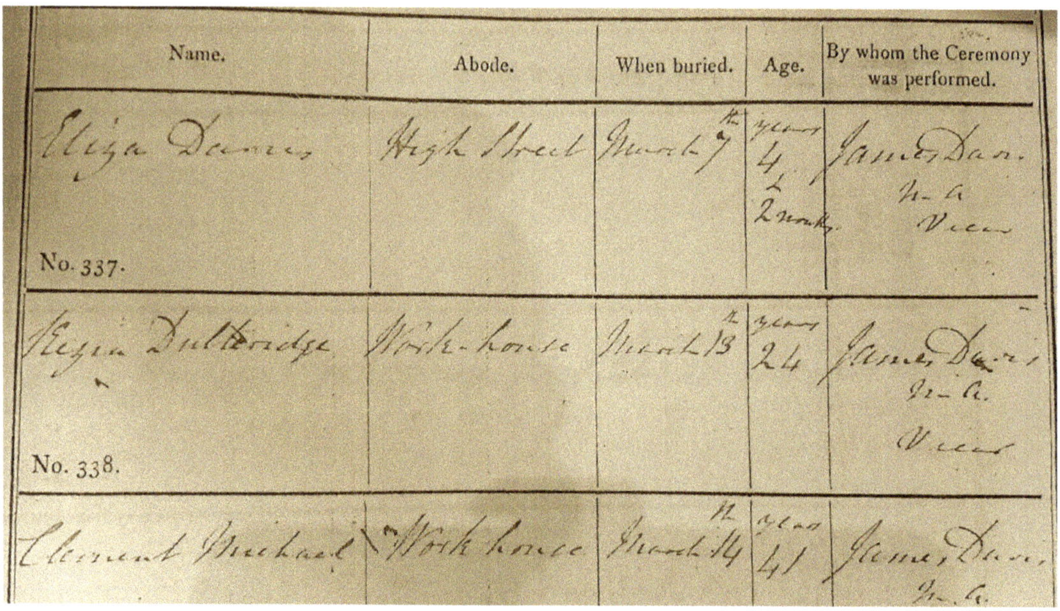

Name.	Abode.	When buried.	Age.	By whom the Ceremony was performed.
Eliza Davies No. 337.	High Street	March 7th	years 4 & 2 weeks	James Davies M.A. Vicar
Kezia Dutheridge No. 338.	Work-house	March 13th	years 24	James Davies M.A. Vicar
Clement Michael	Workhouse	March 14th	years 41	James Davies M.A.

Parish records of St Mary's in Chepstow, showing the burial of Kezia Dutheridge. Unfortunately, although Monmouthshire Council state paupers' graves are marked with a 'P', research for this book discovered the exact location appears to be unknown. (Kind thanks to St Mary's for loan of the register book)

Chepstow Board School.

Remaining building of the workhouse's front elevation – now a nursery.

Remaining building of the workhouse on the right at the junction of Mounton Road and Regent Way.

Remaining wall of the workhouse main block on Regent Way.

6. Crime and Punishment

By 1524, the Town Gate had been rebuilt by the Earl of Worcester and handed over to the Burgesses of Chepstow to be used as a prison or lock-up house. In 1850, a prison inspector's report notes how lax the security is, with some prisoners simply removing bricks to escape and others picking the lock. The report carries on to say it is one simple room being 12 foot by 9 foot, with a bench and no bedding – not even straw. Female prisoners were kept at nearby taverns if male prisoners were present but even they could get away easily as the officers watching them were lax in their duties. It is worth bearing in mind that these were not police officers as we know them today. In fact, a 'police officer' didn't exist until 1856, before then it was up to parish constables to keep law and order, who were often unpaid.

In 1850, the Town Gate is noted as being in one of the less pleasurable parts of Chepstow and surrounded by vagrants and thieves. Stand at the Town Gate today and imagine no traffic, no lighting and no modern architecture, and you can almost picture the eeriness of it.

In 1609 it became law for each county, including Monmouthshire, to have their own house of correction and for Justices of the Peace (magistrates) to be responsible for them, in turn reporting to the county quarter sessions. Crimes committed in Chepstow were heard at Shire Hall in Monmouth and criminals were imprisoned at Monmouth Gaol. Originally a lock-up in Monnow Bridge Gatehouse, Monmouth Gaol was built in 1790, with some alterations in 1820.

DID YOU KNOW?
The crank device used as hard labour punishment could be tightened by the prison wardens to make it more difficult to turn. This is how the nickname 'screws' came about for prison wardens.

People were imprisoned for acts that today would not be considered worthy of such punishment. Stealing a loaf of bread, for example, could give you fourteen days' hard labour. 'Hard labour' included treadmills or treadwheels where prisoners would have to walk on this device under guard and in silence. Some prisons used the device to make flour for bread and inmates would earn some money, but generally the treadwheel was simply just walked on. According to the Victorian Crime and Punishment website, the treadwheel, became a pet hate of prisoners. Another device used for a hard labour

Above: Monmouth Gaol, *c.* 1820 – the toll house on the left still survives today on Hereford Road.

Left: A blue plaque on the remaining gatepost of old Monmouth Gaol.

sentence was that of the crank, a handle that the prisoner had to turn thousands of times a day. Children were no exception either: the MonGenes website, for example, shows a picture of a twelve-year-old boy sentenced to ten days' hard labour and three years in a reformatory for stealing bread and cheese. In 1871, there is a report of a seventeen-year-old female in Chepstow convicted of stealing 'wearing apparel' and sentenced to twenty-one days of hard labour. Offences appear to be mainly larceny (theft), vagrancy, assault, riots. The offenders were usually male, with female crimes usually involving prostitution or theft. These 'hard labour' punishments were not abolished until 1898.

In 1869, Monmouth Gaol was closed down and inmates moved to the New Gaol in Usk, where today's prison still survives. Monmouth Gaol was demolished in 1884, with only the gatehouse surviving. The gatehouse roof used to be flat and is where the hangings took place. Today it is a Grade II-listed building.

On 11 September 1841, the *Monmouthshire Merlin* ran a tragic story entitled 'Murder in Chepstow':

> Our usually quiet town has lately been the scene of shocking depravity, resulting in the death of a young female, who had left her father's roof, to dwell with bad characters. The following particulars appeared in evidence before a coroner's jury, summoned to enquire into the circumstances connected with the death of Sarah Sophia Fleming. It appeared that the deceased who was between 19 and 20 years of age, quitted her father's house, at Whitsuntide last, through the solicitations of Benjamin James and his sister, at Chepstow, and from that time has led a depraved life, and almost wholly supported Benjamin James by the proceeds arising from her prostitution. On Sunday evening, the 29th lilt., she and a female companion in misfortune were walking on the Chepstow Bridge, at hall-past nine, when they met three young men who were going to their homes, near Tutshill. At the foot of the bridge these young men were joined by the two girls and Benjamin James; and shortly afterwards one of the lads (Edmund Jones), and the girl Fleming began to ascend the hill together, followed at a distance by the other female, and the two lads, leaving James alone. James then followed, and overtook the last of the party, but not finding the whole together he lay down upon the grass and called out 'Sal, Sal'. Receiving no answer, he soon got up and proceeded towards the gate at the top of the hill leading into the turnpike road, where he accosted the deceased with 'How be'st Sal?' and immediately got over the gate, and made an attempt to strike her, but missed his aim. Jones here interfered, and collared, and held him for a time, when lie broke loose, and hit Fleming a severe blow on her side, which caused the unhappy girl to cry out bitterly. Jones again engaged bun, and the girl got off a short distance, when Jones tried, without effect, to persuade James to go home, and the girl to return to Chepstow, but Fleming said, 'If I do James will only beat me worse when he catches me' and was crying very bitterly. At length Jones who found entreaties were of no use, released James, who, immediately on being liberated, ran towards the girl; a great noise was then heard. He then struck Fleming with such force on her side, that she fell on her knees; he then laid hold of her hands and dragged her up, when she reeled against the wall; here James lay down, and swore he would murder her by his God. After this Fleming complained very much of being hurt, and entreated James not to strike her again. They then went, and

remained in an out-building, at Chapel- house Farm, near the same place. On Monday morning Fleming complained verv much of her side. They passed that day wandering about, and took up then-abode that night in the neighbourhood of St. Lawrence, under a hay-mow. On Tues, day morning, Sarah Fleming was very ill, had been groaning all night, and being a wet morning they removed to a shed on the opposite side of the road. Here she was very ill, and James being alarmed got her some tea from the town, after obtaining a shilling from the deceased to buy it, who gave it with reluctance, exclaiming, Ben. 'you are always wanting money;' James replied, 'I suppose because you want none, nobody else wants? bull shall buy some tea for you, and beer for myself.' By this time (ten o'clock), the rumour of a girl having been ill-treated reached the ears of constable Magill, who, to his credit, immediately proceeded, with a friend, to the shed, and found the deceased very ill, and accused James of having ill-used her, who replied, 'That's nothing to you, that's only between her and me.' Magill replied, 'I must see to that, and also look for a doctor.' Magill then left the shed, and went in search of Mr. Bradford, surgeon, whom he soon found and took to the shed, but the parties had left. James, for fear of being taken into custody, had induced, or rather forced the girl away to a private retreat near Chepstow Castle, where they remained until evening, the poor girl continuing very ill. that night (Tuesday), James told the girl he was afraid to stop with her, lest he should be taken into custody. The poor girl grew worse, and, by great exertion, at twelve o'clock, reached a lodging-house, in St. Thomas Stree Chepstow, when she took a little ale, was put to bed, continued very ill, all night, and on Wednesday morning, on her father being sent for, she consented to be removed to the Union Workhouse, for she said she should very soon die. Medical aid was instantly obtained, and, on the recommendation of Mr. Bradford, coroner, her deposition was taken by Colonel Lewis, who soon caused James to be apprehended. The poor girl exhibited great fear of James and a certainty of death .and repeatedly accused James of murdering her, and robbing her by cutting off her pocket, which contained twelve shillings. She lingered until Friday afternoon, when death ended her earthly sufferings in the presence of Colonel Lewis, the magistrate. The excitement in the town was considerable. A post mortem examination of the body took place by Dr. Morris on Saturday, and adjourned until Monday, when, after the whole of the evidence had been carefully gone through, a verdict of Wilful Murder, was given against Benjamin James, who had been previously committed to Monmouth Gaol, on a charge of having robbed Fleming of twelve shillings, by cutting off her pocket and abstracting the money.

Such a tragedy, and seemingly quite out of character for Chepstow at this time, judging by various newpaper reports. Benjamin James subsequently had the charge reduced from murder to manslaughter and was imprisoned for a year at Monmouth Gaol.

In November 1900, the following appears in the *County Observer and Monmouthshire Central Advertiser*:

CHEPSTOW. POLICE COURT, MONDAY. Before G. SEYS, Esq. A REFRACTORY INMATE John Dutheridge, was charged with refractory conduct at the Chepstow Workhouse, and with assaulting the master, Mr. Clement Baker, on Saturday. Dutheridge has been very

> troublesome and expensive to the guardians, going constantly in and out, and has been in the asylum. On Saturday he sought re-admission. and upon being questioned and searched a bottle of spirits was found on him. Dutheridge thereupon became violent and struck the master in the face. He was sentenced to 14 days' imprisonment.

A 'refractory' inmate means one who is wilful and unmanageable. This was not the first time Dutheridge had an altercation with the master, Clement Baker: five years previously he had attacked him. In November 1895, the *Evening Express* reported that John Dutheridge attempted to murder the master of Chepstow Workhouse by jumping out on him from a hiding place with an old knife, luckily failing, but wounding the master in the side of the neck. The report states that Dutheridge was unable to comprehend his actions and was committed to the asylum again, after having been there a few times in the past.

With regard to John Dutheridge, whose birth was mentioned in the previous chapter on Chepstow Workhouse, John's history seems to be a sad one and typical of an orphaned child in a workhouse. The Workhouse Board of Guardians were the legal guardians of orphaned children up to the age of sixteen. In the 1861 census, we have an eighteen-year-old John Dutheridge lodging at Butler's Court Farm as an agricultural labourer in Gloucestershire. In 1869, the *County Observer and Monmouthshire Central Advertiser* ran a short piece on a John Dutheridge being 'drunk and riotous' in Raglan and said he was committed to Usk for seven days. In 1878, the *Monmouthshire Merlin and South Wales Advertiser* states a John Dutheridge committed to Chepstow for being

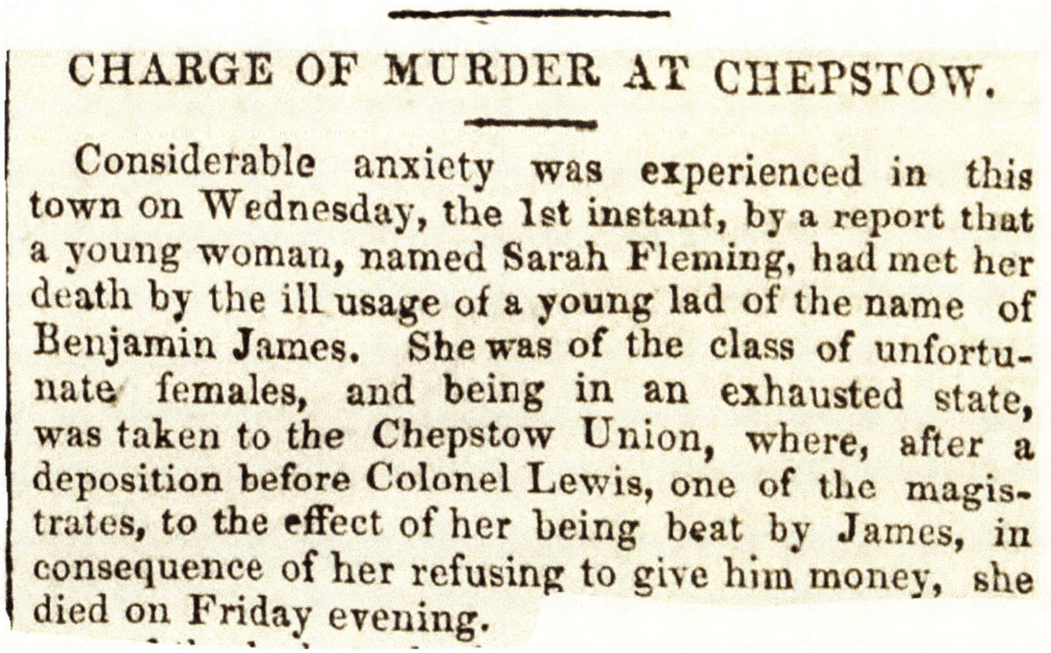

CHARGE OF MURDER AT CHEPSTOW.

Considerable anxiety was experienced in this town on Wednesday, the 1st instant, by a report that a young woman, named Sarah Fleming, had met her death by the ill usage of a young lad of the name of Benjamin James. She was of the class of unfortunate females, and being in an exhausted state, was taken to the Chepstow Union, where, after a deposition before Colonel Lewis, one of the magistrates, to the effect of her being beat by James, in consequence of her refusing to give him money, she died on Friday evening.

The *Glamorgan, Monmouth and Brecon Gazette* and *Merthyr Guardian*, 11 September 1841.

drunk. John doesn't appear again until the census of 1891, which shows him as an inmate at Abergavenny – single, a labourer and aged forty-eight.

Built in 1851 after the Lunacy Act of 1845, Abergavenny was made the county asylum for Monmouthshire, Herefordshire, Breconshire and Radnorshire (the old Marcher lands). It initially held 210 inmates within twelve wards, but by the latter half of the nineteenth century it could hold 1,170 inmates due to extension work over previous years. It was at this time that the catchment area for the asylum was reduced, and it became Monmouthshire Asylum in 1897. In 1930 it became Monmouthshire Mental Hospital and then Pen-y-Val Hospital in 1948, closing its doors in 1996. Many people were incarcerated into asylums for reasons beyond our modern understanding – 'crimes' such epilepsy, female 'troubles' and mania to name a few.

Finally, in 1904, the parish records show the death of a John Dutheridge, aged sixty-one, in Chepstow. It is safe to surmise this life of John Dutheridge is one and the same due to the right age and demographic, plus the repeat readmissions into the asylum and Chepstow Workhouse.

DID YOU KNOW?
Although public whipping as a punishment had been abolished by the 1830s, private whipping in gaols was still allowed until 1848, especially for children who were ordered to be whipped privately in gaol prior to their release.

7. Roads, Rivers, Railways and Bridges

Chepstow has long been a hub of transport and communication, mainly due to its situation at the confluence of the Severn and the Wye. One of the earliest places associated with travel was an area that became known as the Old Passage. This was an ancient route used by the Romans and known as Trajectus Augustus – *trajectus* meaning 'crossing' – that was between Aust in South Gloucestershire and Beachley, two settlements practically facing each other across the Severn. It is thought Aust may take its name from Trajctus Augustus, thus being named after the Second Augusta Legion stationed at Caerleon. Or the name could come from St Augustine, who travelled with a Roman papal party for a conference and to convert Welsh bishops from the old religion to Christianity. This conference included arguing over the correct dates of Easter and became known as Augustine's Oak. Bede, however, writing in around 730 AD, gave a geographical description that does not actually fit Aust, and there have been suggestions it was more likely held at what is now College Green in Bristol.

David Higgins, writing for Bristol and Gloucester Archaeological Society, states that Aust was simply a minor ferry point that sat beneath Aust Cliff, a dramatic cliff that rose at the point on the eastern side of the Severn that, until the Severn Bridge opened in 1966, had given guidance across the water from South Wales over the ages. In fact, Higgins goes onto say that Aust is not mentioned in any Roman documentation and first appears in its modern form in 1546, in John Leland's *The Itinerary*. The Romans never bestowed Augusta on any place other than a *civitas* (such as Caerwent) or on a settlement of upwards of 2,000 inhabitants. Aust has no archaeological evidence of any settlement, other than a late Iron Age temple atop Aust Cliff. Higgins goes on to say that Aust could simply be an Anglo-Saxon derivation of 'east' cliff, as seen by much earlier Irish and Welsh navigators of the Severn Estuary.

DID YOU KNOW?
John Rennie (1761–1821) was an engineer who pioneered designing stone structures to replace wooden ones, notably Waterloo Bridge in London and redesigning docks at Hull and Liverpool.

The GGAT describes the historic River Wye as 'a natural communication corridor ... with an extensive history of human occupation and exploitation'. We've already seen a snapshot of the industry that was associated with the river. Additionally, water-based

Remains of the Old Passage Ferry as it is today. It closed in 1966, not long after the Severn Bridge (seen to the right) was opened. It ran to a similar terminus at Beachley – the whitewashed Ferry Inn is visible in the background of the photograph. A ferry had been running here since Roman times, possibly earlier.

Looking back up the ancient ferry track (the ruins are from the 1960s) from the banks of the Severn Estuary.

Aust Cliff, showing millions of years of geology and providing a point of reference when crossing the Severn Estuary from South Wales.

industries such as limekilns, furnaces, ironworks and wireworks developed at Tintern on the Wye, but there were none similar below Tintern. GGAT notes the geology of the river and states its banks change at Tintern, thus dictating particular industries upon certain points of the Wye Valley.

The Wye as a means of transport changed and reduced dramatically after the development of the turnpike road through the valley in 1829, a route that runs approximately where the modern A466 now is. Tolls were not popular as they were perceived as another form of tax. In his *History of Wales,* Davies notes the appalling condition of Welsh roads and, unlike in France, Britain's roads were not considered the responsibility of the government and only developed over the years as per local demand. Chepstow, with its convenient location on the Severn/Wye estuary, was proof of the importance of river travel as opposed to road. In his book *Medieval Roads and Tracks,* Paul Hindle discussed research that had proven the importance of river travel in medieval times and noted the Severn could have been navigated to Welshpool. This was seen in the success of the Chepstow's medieval port.

There was great poverty in South Wales in the early 1800s and the toll gates became a focus of demonstration and violence, also known as the Rebecca Riots. In his *History of Monmouthshire,* Bradney notes how the lanes leading into Chepstow were widened, straightened and improved in the early nineteenth century, allowing for better and faster coach travel. In 1808, a road was made for ease of travelling from Gloucester to Chepstow via Tutshill.

In the thirteenth century, pavage grants (an early form of what would become tolls) were first mentioned in Letters Patent (official published written orders by the monarch) for the upkeep of a marketplace or town paths, similar to pontage for bridges. In 1530, the Bridges Act came into force due to the constant repairs on wooden bridges: the parish or town in which the bridge was located was responsible for the upkeep, which was enforced by Justices of the Peace. This was where Chepstow Bridge was unique, as two parishes/counties were responsible for the upkeep – Monmouthshire and Gloucestershire.

Then, in 1555, came the Highway Act, which required local people to be 'surveyor of highways' in their parish and be responsible for the upkeep of the roads. In 1663 the first toll road opened – the Great North Road – and the first turnpike was erected on the Hertfordshire section. In his book *Turnpike Roads,* Geoffrey N. Wright states that this new concept of tolls – whereby the cost fell upon the traveller as opposed to the parish – took another thirty years to establish and the first Turnpike Act was introduced by 1700. Turnpike trusts were given powers to borrow money for managing roads and were responsible for repairs – there were a growing number of these trusts throughout the eighteenth century, but they tailed off during the nineteenth century, mainly due to the arrival of the railways. Between 1753 and 1839 over 200 turnpike trusts were authorised in Wales by Parliament. These trusts were responsible for the upkeep of the roads, but were also open to corruption and inefficiency.

DID YOU KNOW?
New South Wales in Australia was named after the Welsh antiquarian and naturalist Thomas Pennant due to his friendship with the chief scientist aboard James Cook's second voyage of 1768–71.

There are many tracks that criss-cross the British countryside from when the populace traversed the rural areas to work the land, roaming for work and moving their animals from place to place, market to market. Many similar ancient trackways were the origin of a number of Britain's roads. The oldest known trackway is the Ridgeway in Wiltshire and is at least 5,000 years old. There are a few walks/rights of way called Ridgeway, which are all elevated and usually long-distance routes that follow higher and therefore drier land. The views along these that the modern-day rambler would find breathtaking played an important role in ancient times: they gave the traveller a commanding view to spot any possible ambush attacks, as well being able to calculate time and distance they were travelling. Ridgeways were used throughout the Bronze Age, Iron Age, after the departure of the Romans, as well as during the time of the Anglo-Saxons and Vikings.

Many modern bridleways and byways for walking are the remains of drover routes. Droving was a respected profession. Not only were they regarded as tough, no-nonsense people due to the control, planning and responsibility of moving large numbers of animals, they had to deal with the financial transactions at the end of each trek. According

Turnpike earned its name from the early design of the gates, which were similar to a *cheval-de-frise* (a medieval anti-cavalry structure, as seen here). They were, quite literally, a pike laid across the road until the toll was paid. Once the fee was paid the pike was moved to allow one's journey to continue. (Courtesy of Brian Stansberry under Creative Commons 3.0).

to an article on droving at walkingworld.com, drovers often set up financial banks, were entrusted to chaperone children who were travelling from well-to-do families, and were the reliable news bearers from farm to farm. Many routes have their beginnings in Wales as well as Scotland, as both these countries had a larger density of cattle rearing. One of the many routes mentioned in sources is the long-haul drover route of North Wales to Smithfield meat market in London. Cattle and sheep (as well as horses, ponies and geese) had to be in good health and fresh on arriving at their destination, so many routes followed waterways as well as high hedges for feeding. *Public Paths* by Graham Bathe notes how routes became established by such things as pine trees planted by farmers who gave permission for the drover and his herd to rest. The last long trek of Welsh sheep occurred in 1900 – they were heading to London.

The Romans gave us more structured roads, some of which are still in use today such as the Fosse Way, which ran from Lincoln to Exeter. Although this could have been built on a previous ancient trackway, it became an important route for trade and military activities. Gloucester became an important and high-status *colonia* known as Glevum, built up on the Severn with close access to the Fosse Way, and possibly became the place where the legions planned the invasion of Wales, eventually settling in Usk and Caerleon. It is in Wales we see the most western-built Roman roads, according to Hugh Davies in his book *Roman Roads in Britain*. He notes that there are no signs of Roman road construction

Left: Welsh Drover statue in Llandovery, which was once one of the busiest drover towns in Wales. (Courtesy of Philip Halling under Creative Commons 3.0).

Below: Example of a typical old drover's route, now a scenic ramble in Ceredigion. (Courtesy of Roger Kidd under Creative Commons 3.0)

in Cornwall despite evidence of forts, and the most westerly roads appear along the south coast of Wales from the legendary Caerleon, through Cardiff and to Carmarthen, continuing westwards, possibly to St Davids.

The Romans didn't appear to have had too much trouble crossing the Severn: the Via Julia is a Roman road that originally ran from Silchester (Hampshire) to Bath – both hugely important Roman towns in the sense of military and settlement. It then ran from Bath towards Abonae (Sea Mills, Bristol) and on to Aust, where a ferry would continue the route across to Caerleon. John Bartholomew, writing in 1887 in a *Gazetteer of the British Isles*, notes how the Via Julia carried onto Carmarthen (then known as Moridunum) a Roman fort and town (most likely the same road mentioned above in the book *Roman Roads in Britain*).

DID YOU KNOW?
Opened in 1886, the Severn Railway Tunnel held the record for the longest underwater tunnel in the world, with 2.25 miles of its length under the Severn Estuary. In 1988, the Saiken Tunnel in Japan opened with an underwater length of 14.5 miles, and in 1994 the Channel Tunnel opened with an impressive 23.5 miles underwater. However, it shows what a feat of nineteenth-century engineering the Severn Tunnel was, holding its record for just over 100 years.

After the Romans left Britain some of their roads survived (the large routes such as the North Road and Fosse Way), but many fell into disrepair and some were lost for good. More locally built roads were nothing more than tracks connecting villages and markets – as they are today – and these didn't necessarily go in a straight line like the Roman ones did. Tracks usually avoided dense woodland, bog areas, wetlands and steep hills – all obstacles the Roman engineers would have tackled head on. Chepstow and the surrounding areas would have been no different.

It is the access road and military route from Gloucester to Caerleon and Caerwent for the Roman legions that gives us the River Wye's original wooden bridge, approximately 1 kilometre north of Chepstow (although some sources state there was an earlier crossing at Tintern). Bradney states in his *A History of Monmouthshire* that 'The Roman road from the direction of Gloucester came down by Tutshill in the parish of Tidenham to the River Wye,' which is very near the current Chepstow Bridge we see today. The Normans built a bridge next to the castle they established in 1067, and although the first mention of it is in 1228 it had probably been around earlier. In 1234, Bradney notes that the bridge needed repair and 'Gilbert de Clare, earl of Pembroke, was given leave to take fifty good oaks, as the king's gift, from the Forest of Dean for repairing Chepstow Bridge.'

John Burrows, in his 2015 *Chepstow Bridges* information leaflet, notes it was a ten-pier wooden bridge consisting of a central stone pillar and had many repairs. A wooden bridge spanned Chepstow's part of the Wye for a little over 500 years where England and Wales connected, and in 1605 a tax levied on the residents of both counties

Roman road map of Britain. (Courtesy of Notuncurious under Creative Commons 3.0)

would pay to maintain the bridge. In 1810, magistrates declared the bridge dangerous, although nothing was actioned due to expense – the engineer John Rennie's quote of £41,890 (approximately £23.5 million today) was deemed too expensive. Rennie had also produced a quote for £15,191 (approximately £855,000 today), which was cheaper due to retaining the old central stone pier at the time. However, a boating accident in 1812

Right: Chepstow Bridge – note the branch, a testament to how high the tidal surge can be.

Below: The 1816 Chepstow Bridge today, looking towards Tutshill, Gloucestershire.

Nineteenth-century ironwork.

with the death of six women and a boatman on a river cruise from Tintern spurred the magistrates into action and the cheaper iron bridge design was put out to tender. In 1814, John Rastrick of Hazeldine and Rastrick Iron Foundry in Bridgnorth, Shropshire, won the contract and designed and built the bridge we see today for £17,850 (approximately £993,000 today).

South Wales Railway (Rheilffordd De Cymru) was originally planned to meet the need to commute coal from the South Wales valleys to London (we have already seen how the coal industry was a death knell for Chepstow Port), as well as to connect to Fishguard and onwards to transatlantic trade via Ireland. However, it didn't quite work out that way: most of the original South Wales Railway line is still used today, after merging with Great Western Railway in 1863.

DID YOU KNOW?
The opening of Chepstow's Iron Bridge in 1816 had been overshadowed somewhat by the opening of the world's largest iron bridge – Vauxhall Bridge in London – only two months previous. Chepstow was one of ten iron bridges built worldwide before 1830, yet only Chepstow remains and is still functional.

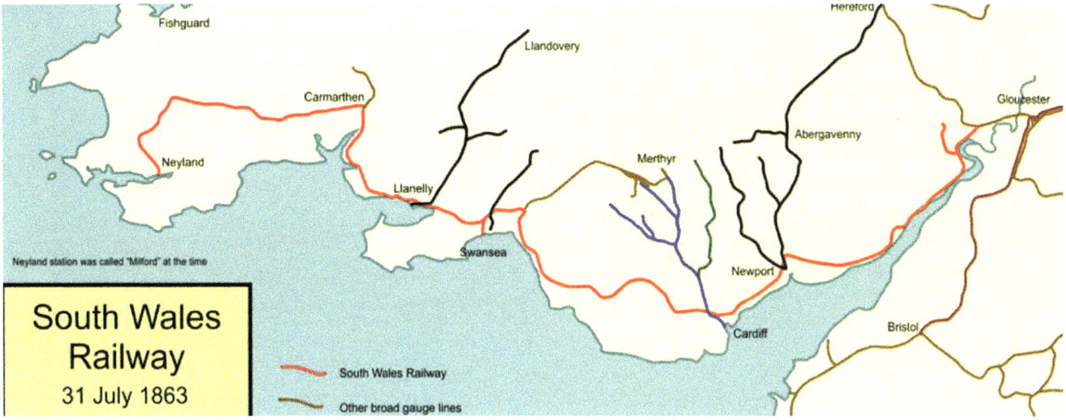

South Wales Railway line. (Courtesy of Afterbrunel under Creative Commons 3.0)

The width of the tidal River Severn stopped any building of a direct railway line from London to Wales. The new journey would head up to Gloucester via the Great Western Railway where the Severn was narrow enough for a bridge. The proposals in 1844 saw a bridge across the Severn originally between two Gloucestershire villages – Fretherne and Awre. However, local people were disappointed the line would not run through Monmouth and the Admiralty (a government office known as Office of the Admiralty and Marine Affairs, an early form of today's Ministry of Defence) objected.

In 1850, the first line of the South Wales Railway opened between Chepstow and Swansea. Initially, if one wished to go further into England and/or up to Gloucester, one had to disembark at Chepstow station to cross the River Wye road bridge as there was a delay in the building of Chepstow Railway Bridge across the Wye. This was completed in 1852 to a radical design by the famous and innovative engineer Isambard Kingdom Brunel and the second line of the railway, Gloucester to Chepstow, opened the same year. After bringing a second track across the bridge at Chepstow in 1853, the journey time from London to Swansea was reduced from fifteen hours by road or ferry, to just five hours by rail.

Brunel's famous design for Chepstow Railway Bridge was the forerunner of his Royal Albert Bridge over the River Tamar in Cornwall. Chepstow Bridge is Grade II listed, despite being replaced (apart from the original iron supports) in 1962.

DID YOU KNOW?
Bob Dylan was photographed waiting for the ferry at Aust in 1966, shortly before it closed down. He was en route to play a gig at Cardiff after being booed in Bristol for playing an electric guitar.

Chepstow Railway Bridge, *c.* 1850. (Ccourtesy of Afterbrunel under Creative Commons 3.0)

Chepstow Railway Bridge today.

Above: Bob Dylan, 1966.

Right: Approximately the same spot today where Dylan stood facing the camera. The image is facing back up the flagstone path to the main Aust Road, with remains of the café and ticket office to the left. The old coaching inn named Old Passage House is in the background.

8. Nathaniel Wells and Piercefield House

In 1749, a member of a wealthy Cardiff family named William Wells (1730–94) emigrated to the British colonial island of St Kitts, becoming a wealthy plantation owner and slave trader. Bradney, in his *A History of Monmouthshire*, notes that the Wells were an old family of Cardiff, holding positions such as baliffs and goldsmiths and mentions an alderman in 1720, who Bradney hints at being the father of Chepstow's Nathaniel Wells. Not long after arriving in St Kitts, William's British wife died and William fathered approximately six children by slave mothers. However, William must have treated them well as the sources show how he looked after them financially and acknowledged his children.

William's eldest and only surviving son was a boy called Nathaniel, whose mother, Joardine (nicknamed Juggy), was one of William's house slaves. When William passed away from dropsy (oedema) in 1794, Nathaniel was only fifteen and too young to inherit. In his father's will provision was made for him to attend school in England and at twenty-one he'd inherit his father's wealth. William Wells appears to have been close to his brothers Revd Robert Wells and Nathaniel Wells Esquire of London, as noted in his last will and testament, dated 10 July 1789, courtesy of the National Archives:

> The remainder of my Estate both real and personal whatsoever and wheresoever I give unto my Natural and Dear Son Nathaniel Wells whose mother is my woman Juggy and who is now in England for his Education and at School at Newington near London and under the care of his Uncle my Brother Nathaniel Wells Esquire of London, and to his heirs for ever on his attaining the age of twenty one years and which will be on the the [sic] 10th. Day of September in the year one thousand Eight hundred but should he not live to the said 10th Day of September one thousand Eight hundred I then give it to my said two Brothers the Reverend Robert Wells and Nathaniel Wells and their heirs for ever to be equally divided between them.

Upon his death, William said:

> I do hereby give Freedom unto my house Negro women Hannah Juggy Gotto and Kate and I do hereby release them from Slavery and I do hereby give unto my said Hannah and Juggy the annual sum of sixty pound Sterling to each of them during their natural lives to be paid unto each of them half yearly I also give to my said Hannah her Negro woman present and all her Children I give to my said Gotto and Kate above mentioned the annual Sum of twenty pounds Sterling to each of them during their natural lives to be paid unto each of them half yearly I do hereby give Freedom to my Mullatto woman Sue Wells and I give her also twenty pounds Sterling to be paid her annually during her natural life half yearly I do hereby give Freedom to my Mullatto Man Simon to my

> houseboy Fill and to Christian and I Coaser my two Drivers and I give to each of them the annual Sum of twenty pounds Sterling during their natural lives to be paid unto each of them half yearly I give unto my natural Daughter Elizabeth whose mother was named Perrin the annual Sum of one hundred and Fifty pounds Sterling during her natural life to be paid her half yearly and I give her also the sum of two thousand and five hundred pounds Sterling I give unto my natural Daughter Ann the Child of Sue Wells the sum of one hundred and fifty pounds Sterling during her natural life to be paid her half yearly and I give her also the Sum of three thousand and five hundred pounds Sterling payable to her when she attains the age of twenty one years I give unto my Natural Daughter Mary Ann whose mother is named Sarah the Annual Sum of one hundred and Forty pounds sterling to be paid half yearly during her natural life and also the further Sum of one thousand pounds.

This was the exception rather than the rule of the day. And so began the extraordinary life of Nathaniel Wells, son of a white British slave owner and a black house slave, who, despite the odds, managed to rise in society, well-respected and noted as a true gentleman of the day. Frustratingly, there appear to be no portraits of Nathaniel available. Colonel Mark Wood, who sold Piercefield estate to Nathaniel in 1802, was heard to say: 'A West Indian of large fortune, a man of very gentlemanly manners, but so much a man of colour as to be little removed from a Negro.' In her blog on Nathaniel Wells Jan Marsh notes that this gives the impression that manners and colour were not considered one and the same and it is perhaps for reasons such as this that Nathaniel never commissioned his own portrait.

Nathaniel decided to stay in Britain after his education and in 1801 the wealth inherited from his father was £200,000, approximately £10.5 million today. In this year he also married Harriet Este, the only daughter of Charles Este, George II's royal chaplain. After her death, Nathaniel married Esther Owen in 1823. Most sources agree he had twenty children altogether – ten by each wife.

DID YOU KNOW?
Nathaniel Wells was only the second mixed-race person to hold a commission in the British Army. The first, a Captain John Perkins, was an officer in the Royal Navy in the late 1700s and there wouldn't be another until the early 1900s: Walter Tull. Tull's grandfather had been a slave in Barbados and his brother Edward was the first mixed-race person to qualify as a dentist in the UK.

In 1802, Nathaniel Wells bought Piercefield House for £90,000 – approximately £6.2 million today. His standing in society rose and in 1804 he became the churchwarden for St Arvan's, a position he held for forty years. In 1806, he took the oath as a Justice of the Peace and in 1818 he was sworn in as High Sheriff of Monmouthshire, the first mixed-race person to hold the elevated role (and possibly the first mixed-race person to be a Justice of the Peace). As sheriff of the county, he was the Crown's representative in upholding and administering local law, justice and organising elections. An article on the website www.scholastic.co.uk noted that there is no evidence to show Nathaniel was ever the victim of prejudice or discrimination; the only comments on his colour, like the one above, were used to describe him, not to ridicule him. Bearing in mind he was in an unusual position, none of which had probably been seen before, especially in high society, the evidence points towards him being a popular, fair and likeable country gentleman.

Having many children, the Wells family often got mentions in local newspapers. However, Nathaniel had his fair share of tragedy. *The Cambrian* ran a 'Family Death Notice' on 12 April 1823: 'At Piercefield, Mr Wm Wells, eldest son of Nathaniel Wells Esq.of that place. He sustained a long and painful affliction with such patience and resignation to the will of God as evinced in the state of his mind.'

On 19 November 1836, *The Monmouthshire Merlin* ran a 'Family Notice' announcing the wedding of Grace Emily Georgiana, fourth daughter of Nathaniel Wells Esq., at St Arvan's Church to a Mr George Watkins of Chepstow. This is the same George Watkins (a surgeon) mentioned briefly in the earlier chapter regarding his ownership of Gwy

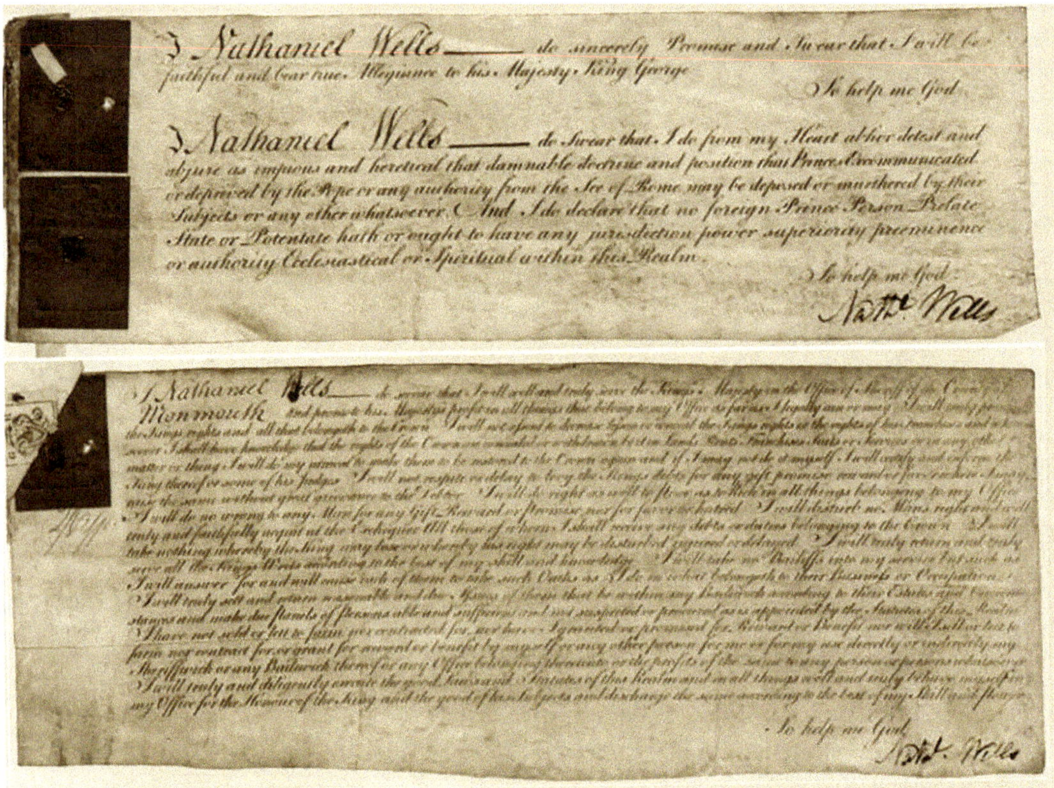

I Nathaniel Wells ——— do sincerely Promise and Swear that I will be faithful and bear true Allegiance to his Majesty King George

So help me God

I Nathaniel Wells ——— do Swear that I do from my Heart abhor detest and abjure as impious and heretical that damnable doctrine and position that Princes Excommunicated or deprived by the Pope or any authority from the See of Rome may be deposed or murthered by their Subjects or any other whatsoever. And I do declare that no foreign Prince Person Prelate State or Potentate hath or ought to have any jurisdiction power superiority preeminence or authority Ecclesiastical or Spiritual within this Realm.

So help me God

Nathl. Wells

Oath of Nathaniel Wells being sworn in as Sheriff of Monmouthshire in 1818. (Courtesy of National Archives under Open Government Licence V3.0)

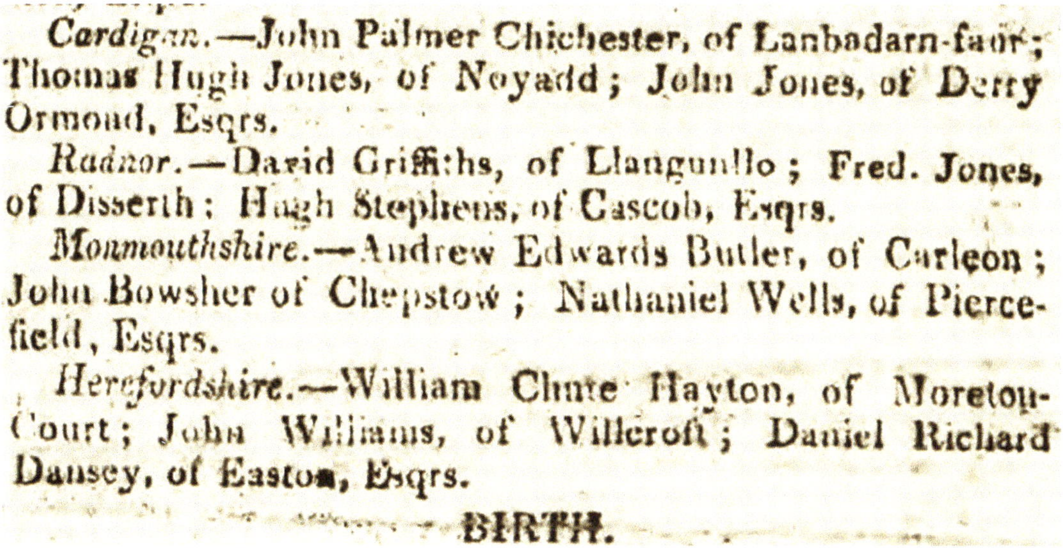

Cardigan.—John Palmer Chichester, of Lanbadarn-faur; Thomas Hugh Jones, of Noyadd; John Jones, of Derry Ormond, Esqrs.

Radnor.—David Griffiths, of Llangunllo; Fred. Jones, of Disserth; Hugh Stephens, of Cascob, Esqrs.

Monmouthshire.—Andrew Edwards Butler, of Carleon; John Bowsher of Chepstow; Nathaniel Wells, of Piercefield, Esqrs.

Herefordshire.—William Chute Hayton, of Moreton-Court; John Williams, of Willcroft; Daniel Richard Dansey, of Easton, Esqrs.

BIRTH.

Above: *The Cambrian* newspaper announcing new sheriffs, November 1817. Note under 'Monmouthshire' the name of John Bowsher of Raglan Lodge is mentioned in an earlier chapter, as well as that of Nathaniel Wells.

Right: Seal of Nathaniel Wells. (Courtesy of National Archives under Creative Commons 3.0)

House. Tragically, in 1841, there is another notice announcing her death in Chepstow from scarlet fever, after only a few days of illness. There is mention of Harrietta Maria, a third daughter, marrying in 1843 and then on 26 February 1844, *The Monmouthshire Merlin* ran a 'Family Notice': 'Nathaniel Armstrong Wells, eldest son, marries Georgiana Lucy of Westbury in Bucks.' Only two years later, on 26 March 1846, we have a 'Death Notice' in another paper stating the passing of a Nathaniel Armstrong Wells, eldest son of Nathaniel Wells Esq. While families such as these usually gave their children same names, it is highly plausible that this 'eldest son' were one and the same.

Nathaniel Wells never returned to St Kitts but, like many other absentee plantation owners, had managers on his estates there overseeing the business and the slaves. The Slavery Abolition Act came into force in 1833 and Dr Nick Draper (quoted on Jan Marsh's blog, Nathaniel Wells) stated that enslavers were entitled to a share of a £20 million compensation fund, although the enslaved in the Caribbean received nothing.

Half of this compensation fund was awarded to absentee holders, of which Nathaniel Wells was one. On 13 August 1837, Nathaniel's claim of £1,400 was honoured (approximately £110,000 today).

Due to failing health, Nathaniel Wells retired to No. 9 Park Street in Bath where he passed away in 1852. He was said to be worth £100,000, around £9.7 million today.

DID YOU KNOW?
Nathaniel Wells was the first mixed-race person to hold the title of High Sheriff (of Monmouthshire).

Piercefield

There was possibly a dwelling at Piercefield long before the ruins of where the current Piercefield House now stand, just along from St Arvan's by the River Wye. Bradney, in his *History of Monmouthshire*, notes that according to Welsh pedigrees by the medieval genealogist Lewis Dwnn, a certain Sir Pyrs ap Andrew Wollff built a house on this site before the Conquest in 1066. In the same pedigree, a Meurig Wolff marries Helen, the daughter of Sir John Persffield of Persffield, and the pedigree first mentions the surname Walter in 1270. The spelling has altered over time: Pyrs, Persffield, Piercewell and Peerswell. GGAT note how the area has archaeological evidence of prehistoric defended settlements around the ancient woodland of Piercefield – two Iron Age settlements known as Piercefield Wood Camps are scheduled monuments. GGAT also note how Piercefield Park contains ancient woodland, prehistoric defensive archaeology and post-medieval industrial features such as quarries and limekilns.

William Coxe, writing *An Historical Tour in Monmouthshire* in 1802, stated that Piercefield had long been the property of the Walter family and describes an old stone chimney in the servants' quarters that had a carving of the family coat of arms with the date '1553' inscribed.

Generations of Walter(s) ownership came to an end in 1727 when a John Walters sold the estate to Thomas Rous, a director of the East India Company, for the princely sum of £3,366. In 1740, Colonel Valentine Morris, son of an Antiguan sugar planter and merchant, purchased Piercefield for £8,250 and claimed to be descended from the Walter family by a marriage in the sixteenth century. By 1753, Valentine's son – also called Valentine Morris – landscaped the estate with woodland walks and viewpoints over the Wye. The area was born in a time when tourism was in its infancy and helped elevate the status of the Wye Tour. This is a tour that had poets such as Coleridge and Wordsworth writing at their most passionate due to the natural, unspoilt beauty along the River Wye, of which Piercefield Park was a part. The Wye Tour (popular between 1782 and 1850) became extremely popular during the Napoleonic Wars (1803–15) when the customary European Grand Tour of the wealthy was not an option. The Wye Tour was inadvertently started by a wealthy rector in 1745 who took some guests on a boat trip from the rectory at Ross-on-Wye – thus began the Wye cruise, with sights such as Symonds Yat, Goodrich Castle and Tintern Abbey. In 1782, Revd William Gilpin, whose readership included George III, published his writings *Observations on the River Wye*, which made the Wye Tour ever popular. Chepstow was the final destination of the Wye Tour and there would have been a pier at the port area for passengers to disembark and make their own way back to their homes.

Looking north up the Wye from the Old Wye Bridge. The castle's Great Tower can just be seen on the left, near where passengers would have disembarked from the Wye Tour.

A Chepstow Heritage Trail plaque in The Back.

A Durham banker named George Smith purchased Piercefield in 1784/5 for £26,200 and it was he who commissioned Sir John Sloane, professor of architecture, to remodel the house. Sloane, the son of a brick maker, favoured the neoclassical design and it is mostly this style that the ruins visible to the modern eye are currently in. In 1794, Smith sold the estate due to financial difficulties and the 2,042 acres were sold via auction to Colonel Mark Wood, a British Army Officer, engineer and MP. He added wings to the house and then sold to Nathaniel Wells Esq., who added to the park by buying land on the Gloucester side of the Wye, bringing the estate to 3,000 acres. After Nathaniel died in 1852, John Russell, High Sheriff of Monmouth, bought the estate in 1855/6 after leasing it previously.

In 1861, John Russell sold Piercefield to form a trust fund for families affected by the explosion in his Risca colliery, which claimed 146 lives. Piercefield estate was purchased by Henry Clay, banker and brewer, and in 1874 his son – also called Henry – inherited the estate where he lived until his death in 1921. After being sold to a local consortium of South Wales gentry and business partners, Chepstow Racecourse was developed (there was horse racing at St Arvans already at this time) and opened for its first race in August 1926. It is still a national horse racing venue to this day, despite being known as RAF Chepstow during the Second World War. Unfortunately, despite several attempts to restore the house and being a Grade II-listed building, Piercefield House still stands in ruins to this day.

Piercefield House by George Eyre Brooks, 1840.

Piercefield House, *c.* 1920.

Piercefield House in 2017. (Courtesy of Andy Walker under Creative Commons 3.0)

Wordsworth wrote 'Lines composed a few miles above Tintern Abbey' while partaking of the Wye Tour in 1798:

Five years have passed; five summers, with the length
Of five long winters and again I hear
These waters, rolling from their mountain-springs
With a soft inland murmur. Once again
Do I behold these steep and lofty cliffs,
That on a wild secluded scene impress
Thoughts of more deep seclusion, and connect
The landscape with the quiet of the sky.

Sketch of the approach to Chepstow Castle by artist Lisa Wyatt. (Courtesy of Lisa Wyatt of Wyatt Sisters Illustration)

Another view of Chepstow Castle from Castle Dell.

Colour map of Chepstow's history.